# Un chien andalou

**CINÉ-FILES: The French Film Guides**
Series Editor: Ginette Vincendeau

From the pioneering days of the Lumière brothers' Cinématographe in 1895, France has been home to perhaps the most consistently vibrant film culture in the world, producing world-class directors and stars, and a stream of remarkable movies, from popular genre films to cult avant-garde works. Many of these have found a devoted audience outside France, and the arrival of DVD is now enabling a whole new generation to have access to contemporary titles as well as the great classics of the past.

The **Ciné-Files French Film Guides** build on this welcome new access, offering authoritative and entertaining guides to some of the most significant titles, from the silent era to the early twenty-first century. Written by experts in French cinema, the books combine extensive research with the author's distinctive, sometimes provocative perspective on each film. The series will thus build up an essential collection on great French classics, enabling students, teachers and lovers of French cinema both to learn more about their favourite films and make new discoveries in one of the world's richest bodies of cinematic work.

Ginette Vincendeau

Published Ciné-Files:
*Alphaville* (Jean-Luc Godard, 1965) – Chris Darke
*Amelie* (Jean-Pierre Jeunet, 2001) – Isabelle Vanderschelden
*Casque d'or* (Jacques Becker, 1952) – Sarah Leahy
*Cléo de 5 à 7* (Agnès Varda, 1962) – Valerie Orpen
*La Grande Illusion* (Jean Renoir, 1937) – Martin O'Shaughnessy
*La Haine* (Mathieu Kassovitz, 1995) – Ginette Vincendeau
*La Règle du jeu* (Jean Renoir, 1939) – Keith Reader
*La Reine Margot* (Patrice Chereau, 1994) – Julianne Pidduck
*Le Corbeau* (Henri-Georges Clouzot, 1943) – Judith Mayne
*Les Diaboliques* (Henri-Georges Clouzot, 1955) – Susan Hayward
*Nikita* (Luc Besson, 1990) – Susan Hayward
*Rififi* (Jules Dassin, 1955) – Alastair Phillips
*Un chien andalou* (Luis Buñuel, 1929) – Elza Adamowicz

# Un chien andalou

(Luis Buñuel and Salvador Dalí, 1929)

Elza Adamowicz

Published in 2010 by I.B.Tauris & Co Ltd
6 Salem Road, London W2 4BU
175 Fifth Avenue, New York NY 10010
www.ibtauris.com

Distributed in the United States and Canada Exclusively by Palgrave Macmillan
175 Fifth Avenue, New York NY 10010



ISBN: 978 1 84885 056 9
eISBN: 978 0 75569 773 1
ePDF: 978 0 85771 127 4

A full CIP record for this book is available from the British Library
A full CIP record is available from the Library of Congress

Library of Congress Catalog Card Number: available

# Contents

What we ask of the cinema is the impossible,
the unexpected, dreams, surprise, which efface the
baseness in souls and throw them enthusiastically
onto the barricades and into adventures.
Robert Desnos

Cave canem... Beware of the dog, it bites.
Jean Vigo

# Introduction: It's dangerous to look inside

In 1929 Buñuel and Dalí produced a seventeen-minute film *Un chien andalou.* When it was first screened it was considered as 'a desperate, passionate call to murder' (Luis Buñuel), a film of 'adolescence and death' (Salvador Dalí), 'that extraordinary film… penetrating so deeply into horror' (Georges Bataille), 'a magnificent crime' (Benjamin Fondane), a film of 'witticism and harmless onanism' (Raymond Aron), 'a tiny little shit of a film' (Federico García Lorca), 'a gob of spit in the face of art' (Henry Miller). Produced from a script said to be based on two dream images – a woman's eye slit by a razor, ants emerging from a hole in a man's hand – the film shocked audiences at its first showing in Paris in June 1929. It ran for eight months at the Studio 28 in Montmartre.

What remains of the scandal provoked at its first screening? Dalí and Buñuel progressed from the *enfants terribles* of Surrealism to iconic figures of mainstream European culture. Their film, first seen in terms of surrealist subversion, was later assimilated into Buñuel's reputation as a major European auteur and into Dalí's spectacular productions of onanistic-oneiric paintings. As an icon of film history, *Un chien andalou* continues to provoke and annoy, attract or alienate viewers: as one critic comments, 'this dog has hardly had its last bark' (Thiher 1979: 24). Its eye-slitting sequence, its disjunctions and non-sequiturs, its use of free association and dreamlike images have influenced major film-makers from Alfred Hitchcock to David Lynch. While this was not the first film to portray the violent mutilation of the body – Méliès' *Histoire d'un crime / A Desperate Crime* (1906) had already shown such images in the burlesque mode, while D.W. Griffith's *Intolerance* (1916) used the violation of the body to denounce fanaticism – *Un chien andalou* was among the first films to use close-up to represent a violent act. The film has been considered as the canon for surrealist cinema, the model for American independent film, the first instance of gore cinema. It has inspired both praise and scorn, lyrical responses and weighty analysis, its import has been alternately overstated and underestimated, its subversive nature constantly reasserted or denied. The radical montage techniques used – fast editing, incongruous juxtapositions, disjunctive narrative – have now been banalized in video clips and advertising.

Critical responses to the film have ranged from the dithyrambic to the dismissive, the lyrical to the clinical, the psychological to the psychoanalytical.[1] Film critic Philip Drummond (1997: 56) contends that the film has been retrieved by the 'adulatory reductivism' it has been subjected to in the vast critical literature which he claims has distorted and flattened the film 'into crude sub-Freudian and sub-Marxist socio-erotic allegory'.[2] However, the aim of critical discourse is precisely to continuously rewrite and hence displace a text. In this perspective, the present study will argue that *Un chien andalou* is a dynamic text constantly transformed in relation to the ever-changing cultural and ideological contexts within which it is re-viewed.

A brief overview of critical writings on the film will establish the diverse theoretical parameters within which it has been analysed. Early commentators read the film largely in the context of Surrealism: their texts are either poetic, a subjective response to the effect rather than the meaning of the film, in which the style of the film is often mimicked in a form of celebratory mimesis, for example via an automatic or collage text (Desnos 1929, Péret 1952); or critical, analysing the film in terms of surrealist aesthetics and ethics, focusing on the themes of desire, violence, revolt, the structures of dream and radical montage (Kyrou 1962, Matthews 1971). Secondly, psychological readings (a popular approach to film analysis from the late 1920s, thanks to the generalization of Freudian dream analysis) focus on the film as an account of the psycho-sexual development of the hero (Mondragon 1949, Piazza 1949). The structuralist /semiotic approach of the 1970s, informed by the work of film theorist Christian Metz, gave rise to the meticulous analysis of particular sequences (Drummond 1977, Williams 1976, Oswald 1981, Marie 1981). Both semiotic criticism and Lacanian theory inform extended psychoanalytical readings (Williams

1981a, Sandro 1987). More recently, critics have discussed the film from an intertextual perspective, situating it within 1920s' film discourses and practices (Fotiade 1995, Powrie 1998). Gender studies are also beginning to inform readings of the film, focusing in particular on the analysis of a 'crisis in masculinity' (Powrie 1998). Finally, recent interpretations have focused on the violence and materiality of the images in readings based on the work of Georges Bataille as a 'dissident' surrealist (Jay 1993, Jones 2004).

Yet the weight of critical discourse has not managed to tame the monster, which continues to foster passionate critical debate, new readings and misreadings, raising issues of ideology, aesthetics, gender, and spectatorship. The instability of its images both invites and resists interpretation: its portrayal of unfixed sexual identity, of the frontiers of the body violated, its inconclusive narratives and ambivalent symbols, continue to produce new readings, while the materiality and viscerality of its images persist in resisting interpretation.

The present study arose from a desire to call into question the often totalizing narratives produced by commentators of the film – starting with Dalí and Buñuel themselves and continuing with several generations of critics – which have often asepticized and packaged the film as the model of surrealist practice in the cinema or as a model psychoanalytical situation. This study explores ways in which the film can be read both within and beyond the concerns of Surrealism. The study is above all a response to the challenge presented to the viewing subject to read it in its very inconclusiveness, its openness to multiple readings, and its very resistance to a single interpretation.

The first chapter re-assesses the anecdotal and largely mythical account of the conception and realization of the film as told by its authors as a model surrealist film, and its reception at its first showing, particularly by the surrealist group. Chapter 2 examines the unresolved tensions within the film between narrative elements and a series of apparently disparate sequences and images, situating the film between melodrama and the cinema of attractions. It considers the question of the viewing subject – as detective or dreamer? – and the allegedly radical nature of a film that was both subversive and nostalgic. Chapter 3 shifts from the consideration of the film as surrealist and 'automatic', the product of individual subjectivities, to an analysis of the film within a wider context, a dense intertextual network. It will be discussed in relation to the shared images of Dalí and Buñuel's student days at the Residencia de Estudiantes in Madrid, to contemporary film melodrama, the 1920s' avant-garde cinema, the films of Fantômas or Méliès, and to fairground entertainment. The last part of the chapter will consider the portrayal of both male and female protagonists within the context of 1920s' gender construction. The conclusion will explore briefly the question of the continuing fascination for the film. Finally, was it a sophisticated response to the avant-garde cinema, a parody of Freudian mise-en-scène, or simply a home movie with its amateurish gaps and inconsequentialities?

## Notes

1 For an overview of critical discourses on *Un chien andalou* see Williams (1996), Powrie (1998).

2 Drummond's extensive article is drawn from '*Un chien andalou*: Text and Context', work-in-progress which has remained unpublished. The preface was to provide an examination of the vast critical literature on the film.

# 1 Producing *Un chien andalou*: myths of origin

> Our imagination, and our dreams, are forever invading our memories; and since we are all apt to believe in the reality of our fantasies, we end up transforming our lies into truths.
> Luis Buñuel

Luis Buñuel:

> When I arrived to spend a few days at Dalí's house in Figueras, I told him about a dream I'd had in which a long, tapering cloud sliced the moon in half, like a razor blade slicing through an eye. Dalí immediately told me that he'd seen a hand crawling with ants in a dream he'd had the previous night.
> 'And what if we started right there and made a film?' he wondered aloud.
> Despite my hesitation, we soon found ourselves hard at work, and in less than a week we had a script. (Buñuel 1984: 103–4)

Salvador Dalí:

> Luis Buñuel one day outlined to me an idea he had for a motion picture that he wanted to make, for which his mother was going to lend him the money. His idea for a film struck me as extremely mediocre [...] I told him that this film story of his did not have the slightest interest, but that I on the other hand had just written a very short scenario which had the touch of genius, and which went completely counter to the contemporary cinema.
> This was true. The scenario was written. I received a telegram from Buñuel announcing that he was coming to Figueras. He was immediately enthusiastic

> over my scenario, and we decided to work out several secondary ideas, and also the title – it was going to be called *Le Chien andalou.* (Dalí 1968: 205–6)

When reading Buñuel and Dalí's accounts of the production of *Un chien andalou*, from script to scenario, shooting, first viewing and promotion, it is interesting to consider the contexts of these descriptions, which explain the sometimes shifting, often contradictory, stories of the making of the film, coloured by subsequent events and disputes, and mythified over time. Firstly, the film was made with the aim of opening the door of Surrealism to the two young Spaniards, which explains why the film was cast in an explicitly surrealist mould, and promoted in line with the principles of Surrealism, the zealous (mis)application of surrealist precepts by two model candidates for Breton's movement. Moreover, Buñuel and Dalí fell out in 1930 over the making of *L'Age d'or*, which might explain Dalí's later claims to sole authorship of the concept and his downplaying of Buñuel's role in writing the script and shooting the film. Since such accounts privilege individual or intersubjective elements over collective sources, giving priority for example to the role of dream images and an alleged automatism in the writing of the screenplay, they wilfully obscure the cultural contexts of the film's production, and in particular the specifically cinematic borrowings and quotations. This wider intertextual framework of the film will be explored in chapter 3. The present chapter will focus on the conception, realization and reception of *Un chien andalou* as told by Buñuel, Dalí and the surrealist group, in accounts which determined to a large extent subsequent interpretations of the film as quintessentially surrealist.[1]

## From scenario to screen: a close collaboration

Buñuel and Dalí met in 1920 as students at the Residencia des Estudiantes in Madrid. Buñuel had enrolled in 1917 for a degree in agronomy which he soon abandoned to study literature and philosophy, graduating in 1924. Dalí registered in 1920 at the Academy of Fine Arts. By January 1929, when they wrote the screenplay, Buñuel had had extensive experience as a film critic, programmer and assistant, while Dalí was becoming an established artist and had written articles on film and photography (see chapter 3 for further details). Buñuel produced *Un chien andalou* after two uncompleted film projects. His original idea for a joint film, based on a short story by Ramón Gómez de la Serna, was rejected by Dalí (1968: 205), who considered it 'extremely mediocre [...] avant-garde in an incredibly naïve sort of way'. The sum of 25,000 pesetas Buñuel received from his mother for this project was to be used to produce their film.

Whose scenario was it? The statements by Buñuel and Dalí quoted at the beginning of this chapter present contradictory accounts of their respective roles in the conception of the film. Buñuel states that the idea for the film originated in two dream images. He underlines the spirit of complicity between the two friends, a complicity that dated from their student days in Madrid. In a letter to their fellow-student Pépin Bello (10 February 1929), Buñuel writes: 'Dalí and I are more united than ever, and we have worked together to make a stupendous scenario, quite without precedent in the history of the cinema. It is something big. You will love it' (Aranda 1975: 58). In later interviews he repeatedly emphasizes the collaborative spirit of the enterprise. He declares to Aranda for example: 'The plot of *Un chien andalou* is a joint work. On some things we worked very closely together. In fact Dalí and I were extremely close during that period [...] But the film is mine' (Aranda 1975: 59). He underlines the collaboration yet again in his memoirs, when he states: 'The amazing thing was that we never had the slightest disagreement; we spent a week of total identification' (Buñuel 1984: 104).[2]

While Buñuel emphasizes the collaborative aspect of the project, Dalí gives himself the lead role, attributing only a bit part to his collaborator. He proclaims on more than one occasion his responsibility for the concept, stating that he had written the scenario before Buñuel's arrival in Figueras – jotted down on the lid of a shoebox! – and claiming that their collaboration concerned only minor elements. Although the original scenario has not survived, Buñuel himself acknowledges Dalí's 'protagonism in the *conception* of the film' in a letter to him (24 June 1929) written shortly after the film's first screening (Gibson 1997: 192). Dalí's repeated claims to be the creator of the scenario can be explained not only by the artist's characteristic self-promotion, but also as the consequence of his later dispute with Buñuel over his contribution to *L'Age d'or*, and over the credits for both *Un chien andalou* and *L'Age d'or*, where Dalí's name does not figure. In a letter to Buñuel dated May 1934, Dalí writes: 'I have just seen *Un chien andalou* at Studio 28, and imagine my *stupefaction,* my *indignation* when I saw that my collaboration is *not* credited *at all.* As you will understand, this is such a gross *moral* and *material* wrong that I immediately put the matter in the hands of a lawyer' (Sánchez Vidal 1988: 202).

According to Buñuel, he and Dalí wrote the script in six days in January 1929 at Dalí's home in Figueras.[3] The point of departure of the script, as recorded in his memoirs quoted above, was the account of two dream images: his own dream linking a cloud passing across the moon to a razor cutting an eye, and Dalí's image of a hand crawling with ants. This, however, contradicts the fact that he had originally attributed both images to Dalí, which would seem to confirm the latter's responsibility for the concept (Bataille 1985: 29).[4] The script was conceived and realized as a montage of dreamlike images and irrational associations. They accepted images and gags that came spontaneously to mind, eliminating all logical associations: 'Our only rule was very simple: no idea or image that might lend itself to a rational explanation of any kind would be accepted. We had to open all doors to the irrational and keep only those images that surprised us, without trying to explain why' (Buñuel 1984: 104). Buñuel gives an example of their working methods:

> We chose only those images that surprised us, and that we both accepted without discussion. For example, the woman grabs a tennis racket to defend herself against the man who wants to attack her. He looks around for something and (now I am talking to Dalí): 'What does he see ?' – 'A flying toad.' – 'Bad !' – 'A bottle of brandy.' – 'Bad !' – 'OK, I see two ropes.' – 'Good, but what is there behind these ropes?' – 'The chap pulls them and falls because he is pulling two large dried marrows.' – 'What else?' – 'Two Marist brothers.' – 'And then?' – 'A cannon.' – 'Bad!' – 'A luxurious armchair. No, a grand piano.' – 'That's great, and on top of the piano, a donkey... no, two rotting donkeys.' – 'Fantastic!' In other words, we conjured up irrational images, without any explanation. (Turrent and Colina 1993: 30–1)

They thus deliberately and programmatically gave priority to striking images and non-sequiturs, rejecting conventional storytelling and any psychological coherence.

Buñuel and Dalí construct their accounts of the production of the script in terms of play, free association and the aleatory, according to a surrealist model, a reference explicitly and repeatedly acknowledged by Buñuel. His statement in the 1929 preface to the script: '*Un chien andalou* would not exist if Surrealism did not exist', is echoed in a text from 1947: '*Un chien andalou* would not have existed if the movement called surrealist had not existed' (Mellen 1978: 151–2). Their interest in Surrealism pre-dated 1929. During the 1920s there were frequent exchanges between the Spanish avant-garde and the Paris surrealist group. Spanish writers and artists went to Paris (a group of painters, musicians and poets, including José María Hinojosa and Gregorio Prieto, met regularly at the Rotonde café in Montparnasse) and Paris surrealists went to Spain to lecture (André Breton in Barcelona in 1922, Louis Aragon at the Residencia in Madrid in April 1925). Articles on Surrealism and translations of surrealist texts were published regularly in Catalan and Spanish avant-garde reviews such as *L'Amic de les Arts*. Buñuel had read Sade, Lautréamont and Jarry, Surrealism's literary precursors. Dalí's 1927 dream-paintings have close affinities with de Chirico and Tanguy's dreamlike landscapes (Ades 1982: 45). Although in 1927 Dalí notes his resistance to the surrealist exploration of the unconscious, stating that he values the clarity and objectivity of the photographic lens over 'the murky processes of the subconscious' (Dalí 1998: 13), in the final issue of *L'Amic de les arts* (March 1929), which he co-edited, Dalí aligns himself wholeheartedly with Surrealism, quoting Breton and referring to Benjamin Péret as 'the most authentic French poet'.

The surrealist technique consciously adopted by Buñuel and Dalí to produce the screenplay was that of automatism. It was written in six days, perhaps in imitation of Breton and Philippe Soupault's collaboration on the first surrealist text *Les Champs magnétiques*, written in 1919 in less than two weeks in very similar conditions of intense collaboration. They freely adapted Surrealism's 'recipe' for producing an automatic text or drawing: take a blank sheet of paper or canvas, clear your mind of any preconceived theme or story, and write or draw anything that comes to mind, guarding against the intervention of reason (Breton 1972: 29–30). Buñuel describes their method:

> We looked for an unstable and invisible balance between the rational and the irrational that would allow us to understand the unintelligible, and unite dream and reality, the conscious and the unconscious, outside of any symbolism [...] It was not a question of linking one image to another in relation to reason or the absence thereof, but simply of finding a continuity that would be satisfying for our unconscious without detriment to the conscious, and, moreover, with no direct relation to the rational. In other words, it was in fact a question of approximating, in theory, what Breton had defined as the precise process of Surrealism. (Aub 1991: 51–2)

This text recalls Breton's definition of Surrealism in his 1924 *Manifesto of Surrealism*:

> SURREALISM. masc. nn. Psychic automatism in its pure state, by which one proposes to express – verbally, by means of the written word, or in any other manner – the actual functioning of thought. Dictation of thought, in the absence of any control exercised by reason, exempt from any aesthetic or moral concern. (Breton 1972: 26)

Moreover, when Buñuel concludes that the images produced 'are as mysterious and inexplicable to the two collaborators as they are to the spectator' (Mellen 1978: 153), he is echoing Breton's comment on *Les Champs magnétiques*: 'To you who write, these elements are, on the surface, *as strange to you as they are to anyone else*' (Breton 1972: 24).

Buñuel and Dalí's conscious and self-consciously mechanistic application of surrealist automatic techniques suggests a playful imitation of automatism. Their combination of spontaneity and lucidity approximates what Dalí was to develop as his 'paranoia-critical method', grounded on the simulation of paranoiac delirium, which replaces automatism's passivity with a more active writing process. The claim that the script was produced quite spontaneously is further called into question when we consider Buñuel and Dalí's extensive knowledge of the cinema, and their experience in film production (Buñuel) and painting (Dalí). Indeed the deliberate eschewing of rational discourse on the one hand, and the pastiche and playful quoting of 1920s' films on the other, suggest that the film was conceived in a dadaist spirit of pastiche and parody as much as a genuine surrealist engagement in the exploration of the unconscious. For surrealist Aldo Kyrou (1962: 16), the film is too ostentatiously automatic: '*Un chien andalou* is a perfectly "automatic" film (and probably the only one), but I believe automatism is necessary when it liberates the self and not when it hides under sometimes flashy adornments. *Un chien andalou* is a crafted film, unlike Buñuel's other films, which are a continuous and uncontrolled outpouring of the "I" '. This would suggest that the script itself is a pastiche of automatism, just as the film, with its conscious and meticulous montage, mimics the fragmentation and absence of logic of dream language.

Dalí and Buñuel read the script to their friend Josep Puig Pujades, a journalist from Figueras, who wrote an article in the local newspaper, *La Veu de l'Empordà* (2 February 1929):

> The entire film is a series of normal events which give an impression of abnormality. They are not arbitrary events, since each has its *raison d'être*, but the way in which they are linked and cut is deeply disturbing [...] You realize that either you must be amazed by everything, no matter how run-of-the-mill or commonplace, or by nothing at all. (trans. Gibson 1997: 192).

The title itself was a source of hilarity for the scriptwriters: 'The title of my present book is *The Andalusian Dog*, which made Dalí and me piss with laughter when we thought of it' (Aranda 1975: 59). It is an absurd title, since the viewer encounters neither a dog nor an Andalusian in the film. They had originally thought of other titles: *Vaya marista / Go Marist*, *El Marista en la Ballesta / The Marist in the Crossbow*, *Es peligroso asomarse al interior/ Dangereux de se pencher en dedans/ It's dangerous to lean inside* (a perversion of the notice on French trains: 'Dangereux de se pencher au-dehors/ Do not lean out of the window), and finally *Un perro andaluz*, the title of a collection of poems Buñuel had written in 1927 but never published. Fellow student and poet Federico García Lorca claimed he was the origin of the title: 'Buñuel's made a little film, just like that!' he used to say, snapping his fingers. 'It's called *An Andalusian Dog*, and I'm the dog!' (Buñuel 1984: 157). According to one critic, the term 'perros andaluces' was a term Buñuel and his fellow-students used disparagingly about a group of Andalusian poets at the Residencia, and the film is read as an account of their sexual ambivalence and their struggle to free themselves from their bourgeois milieu (Aranda 1975: 46). Whatever the truth, the presence of a complex contextual and intertextual network around the title alone suggests that Buñuel's claim that it was invented outside any cultural considerations is difficult to sustain.

The film was shot in just two weeks (2–17 April 1929), at the Paris Billancourt Studios and on location at Le Havre for the final beach sequence.[5] Pierre Batcheff (1901–1932) agreed to play the male lead part. A wellknown actor, the 'French James Dean of the 1920s' (Drummond 1977: 78), he had worked with French film directors Abel Gance, Jean Epstein and Marcel L'Herbier. Buñuel and Dalí were keen to obtain the collaboration of an established actor like Batcheff in order to attract funding.[6] Buñuel had met the actor when he was an assistant to Henri Etiévant and Mario Nalpas on *La Sirène des tropiques* / *The Siren of the Tropics* (1927). On the same set Buñuel had met Simone Mareuil (1903–1954), who played the principal female protagonist in his film. The other parts were played by non-professionals. The androgyne's role was played by Fano Mesan, with her bobbed hairstyle and men's clothes in the *garçonne* fashion of the time. Robert Hommet – 'the young, strong, blonde, square-jawed, German, oozing elegant health', writes Buñuel in a letter to Dali (22 March 1929) – played the part of the new lover on the beach. The Marist priests were played by Catalan anarchist publisher Jaime Miravilles and Dalí, who was replaced by the production manager Marval in the second shot. Buñuel appears in the prologue, then disappears from the set. In the park scene, Dalí and Jeanne Rucar, Buñuel's fiancée, are seen walking away from the camera. Extras for street scenes and the sequence in the park were coopted from a local café. The film's cameraman was Albert Duverger, who had worked on Epstein's *Mauprat* (1926) and *The Siren of the Tropics*, and was to work on the set for *L'Age d'or* the following year. Production designs were by Pierre Schildknecht, and Rucar was in charge of budget and costumes.

The property-man seems to have found the list of props needed for such a short film quite bizarre:

> These were some of the things we asked for: a nude model, for whom he had to find some way of wearing a live sea-urchin under each arm; makeup for Bacheff (sic) in which he would have no mouth, and a second one in which his mouth would be replaced by hairs which by their arrangement would recall as much as possible those of the underarms; four donkeys in a state of decomposition, each of which had to be placed on a grand piano; a cut-off hand, looking as natural as possible, a cow's eye, and three nests of ants. (Dalí 1968: 213)

In fact, Buñuel had written to Dalí in Figueras (22 March 1929) asking him to bring some ants back from Spain, with precise details for their transport, and adding: 'It depends on you whether I'll have to use caterpillars, flies or rabbits in the hole in the hand' (Gibson 1997: 201–2).

Batcheff's Paris apartment was used as the film-makers' base, where the film rushes were screened with a second-hand 35 mm projector (Tual 1978: 102). They followed the script closely, making only a few changes. The shooting script was typed in Spanish, with the precise focal length of lenses for many of the shots (Baxter 1994: 81). Shooting itself appears to have been quite haphazard, if one is to accept Buñuel's comments:

> The filming took two weeks; there were only five or six of us involved, and most of the time no one quite knew what he was doing.
> 'Stare out the window and look as if you're listening to Wagner,' I remember telling Batcheff. 'No, no – not like that. Sadder. Much sadder.'
> Batcheff never even knew what he was supposed to be looking at, but given the technical knowledge I'd managed to pick up, Duverger and I got along famously. (Buñuel 1984: 104)

Although Buñuel states he did not improvise, he did not show his actors the script, preferring to give them what seemed at times rather odd instructions:

> I would simply say to them: 'Now look through the window. An army is marching past.' Or else: 'Over there is a fight between two drunkards.' In fact it tied in well with the scene of the girl playing with the severed hand. The cameraman and technicians had no idea of the script [...] No, I didn't say I was improvising. I left out things [...] but I didn't improvise. I knew more or less what I was going to do. For me the script has always been used as a base. (Turrent and Colina 1993: 33)

While Buñuel is known to have claimed that he was sole responsible for the shooting of the film (Aub 1991: 32), elsewhere he acknowledged Dalí's role: 'The film was 50% of each of us [...] I did the cutting of the eye and the ants in the hand, Dalí did the garden scene and the cocktail shaker bell' (Aranda 1975: 60). However Buñuel played down Dalí's contribution to the shooting, maintaining that Dalí arrived on location a few days before the end of the shoot – a photograph of the cast on the beach at Le Havre where the closing scenes were filmed is evidence that Dalí was indeed present on the set at that point – and that his main contribution was the preparation of the rotting donkeys and two brief appearances on screen

(Buñuel 1984: 104–5). Dalí himself acknowledged Buñuel's role as director and scriptwriter in 1929 (Dalí 1998: 100), but he would later make much of his own contribution, claiming he was a constant adviser throughout the shooting, albeit absent from the studio:

> [Buñuel] undertook, moreover, to take charge of the directing, the casting, the staging, etc [...] But some time later I went to Paris myself and was able to keep in close touch with the progress of the film and take part in the directing through conversations we held every evening. Buñuel automatically and without question accepted the slightest of my suggestions; he knew by experience that I was never wrong in such matters. (Dalí 1968: 205–6)

Dalí (1968: 213) also describes his preparation of the dead donkeys' scene in full gory detail: he gouged out the donkeys' eyes, poured glue over them to give the effect of putrefaction, and exposed their teeth to rhyme with the piano keys.

The film is seventeen minutes long and has 300 shots, each lasting an average of three seconds.[7] Buñuel is credited with the montage, which was carried out with great precision. Brunius (1929: 231) notes 'the simplicity and the perfection at work in the *découpage*, the shooting and the montage, the visible control in the mise en scène'. Fast cutting, established by Griffith in 1913, had become standard film language by the mid-twenties. Several critics have claimed that Buñuel's model was Louis Feuillade's *Fantômas* or *Les Vampires*, whose editing was free from special effects, rather than avant-garde film directors with their technical complexities.[8] However, the film does have unusual camera angles (high-angle shots on the cyclist and androgyne) and special effects (slow-motion shots, dissolves, multiple exposure, superimposed shots), characteristic of 1920s' French avant-garde cinema. Buñuel and Dalí might well have wished to pastiche the elaborate technical effects used by avant-garde directors (see chapter 3 for a discussion of the film as pastiche). To save money, the special effects were achieved at the shooting rather than the editing stage. Dissolves were produced by rewinding the film and refilming on the exposed film (a technique Méliès had used), while fades were achieved by iris closing shots (Baxter 1994: 81). Credits were done in a rush, when Buñuel had already left for Madrid after completing the shooting and editing, which no doubt explains the names misspelt or left out. Actors Simone ('Simonne') Mareuil and Pierre Batcheff ('Batchef') are credited, but neither Buñuel, Mesan, Hommet, Miravilles, Marval nor Dalí appear in the credits.

The debates and contradictions relating to the contributions of Buñuel and Dalí to the scenario, script, shooting and editing of *Un chien andalou* are not limited to the two main protagonists. A number of film historians and critics have downplayed or overrated the contribution of one or the other, a judgement often coloured by the later activities of Dalí or Buñuel. For example, Aranda (1975: 60) is clearly on the side of Buñuel when he claims that, if the film is compared with Buñuel and Dalí's later work, 'not only the cinematographic quality, but also all the positive values of the film are those of Buñuel'. Kyrou (1963: 9) makes a similarly categorical retrospective judgement when he writes passionately about Buñuel's input and scathingly about Dalí's: 'I am convinced that Buñuel and Dalí were aiming at different things. Buñuel sought to catch a glimpse of that incandescent world in which dream and reality mingle in a magnificent gesture of liberation; Dalí hoped to shock the bourgeoisie.' The latter's contribution is allegedly identified in the ostentation and exaggerated symbolism of certain scenes, elementary freudianism and window-display tricks. In contrast, Buñuel's scenes are characterized as 'real cries of revolt', an exploration of 'latent reality' beyond satire, aesthetics and jokes. Buñuel, according to Kyrou, wished to 'push his scalpel-camera into the open wound of real flesh'. Dalí's friend Jaime Miravilles, who played one of the Marist priests, perhaps best assessed the contribution of each when he stated that the original idea was without doubt Dalí's, while Buñuel was largely responsible for the execution of the film (Gibson 1997: 658). More important, however, is the fact that the film was the product not simply of two individuals, but of a cultural and social context, which the film quotes, parodies and subverts, as will be explored in chapter 3.

## Première and reception of *Un chien andalou*

Even the film's première generated conflicting reports. Once it had been edited, Buñuel approached the surrealists Man Ray and Louis Aragon, claiming that *Un chien andalou* was 'perhaps a surrealist film' (Tual 1978:

103). Man Ray agreed to screen the film along with his own film *Les Mystères du château du Dé*, recently completed for the art patron the Vicomte Charles de Noailles, at a private screening at the left-bank art-cinema Studio des Ursulines on 6 June 1929 (Buñuel 1984: 105). According to Buñuel and others, the screening was attended by 'the *tout-Paris* – some aristocrats, a sprinkling of well-established artists [...], the entire surrealist group in toto' (Buñuel 1984: 106). Surrealist Georges Sadoul, however, strongly denies the presence of the surrealists: 'One thing is certain. We were not present as a group to acclaim the film, but went individually and our meeting with Buñuel took place *after* the première which we did not attend' (Sadoul 1962: 14). The contradictions may be explained by some confusion between several screenings of the film in the course of summer 1929.[9] During the first screening, Buñuel stood behind the screen with a gramophone, alternating extracts of Wagner's *Liebestod* from *Tristan und Isolde* and two Argentinian tangos. Fearing hostile audience reaction, he kept stones in his pockets (Buñuel 1984: 106). Witnesses testify to the cool reception of Man Ray's film, contrasting with the prolonged applause after the screening of *Un chien andalou* (Tual 1978: 104).

The script, based on the shooting script, was published in *La Revue du cinéma* and the last issue of *La Révolution surréaliste* (December 1929). Photogrammes of the film were reproduced in July 1929 in *Variétés* and *Les Cahiers d'art*, and in August in *Bifur*. The Vicomte Charles and Marie-Laure de Noailles, to whom Buñuel was introduced through Christian Zervos, editor of *Cahiers d'art*, hosted several screenings in July 1929 in their private Paris cinema Place des Etats-Unis, attended by artistocrats and intellectuals, including Carl Dreyer, Michel Leiris and Léon Moussinac. The film was bought by Jean Mauclaire, director of Studio 28, a new Montmartre art-cinema, where it opened on 1 October 1929 for an eight-month run, in a double bill with a Donald Crisp thriller, *The Cop*, then with Harold Lloyd and Mack Sennett comedies (Baxter 1994: 93).[10] Buñuel received an advance of 1000 francs, and earned a total of about 8000 francs (Buñuel 1984: 108). Other screenings followed, at the International Congress of Independent Cinema held in September in La Sarraz in Switzerland, where, according to Dalí, it was praised by the film director

Sergei Eisenstein, who is alleged to have declared that the film exposed 'the extent of the disintegration of bourgeois consciousness' (Baxter 1994: 100). It was first screened in Spain on 24 October 1929 in a Barcelona film club and in Madrid at the Royalty Cinema. The film was acquired by Raymond Rohauer, one of the principal distributors of the silent cinema for Les Grands Films Classiques. A soundtrack was added in 1960 under Buñuel's supervision, corresponding to the original music played on a gramophone. In 1982, the composer Mauricio Kagel, commissioned by Swiss TV, created a soundtrack for stringed instruments and dog-barks.

Was the film an immediate *succès de scandale*, destroying 'in a single evening ten years of pseudo-intellectual post-war avant-gardism', as Dalí would later claim (1968: 212)? In answering this question it is important to distinguish reviews written when the film was first shown from later comments. The film acquired its reputation as a shocking film largely retrospectively, through association – and often confusion – with the greater scandal caused at the first showing of *L'Age d'or* in 1930 (also screened at Studio 28), and partly as a consequence of the surrealists' enthusiastic promotion of the film.

Several of the critics who viewed the film when it was first screened evoked the powerful assault on the senses. André Delons (1929: 22) for instance notes the violence of its images:

> It is the very first time that images, shot through with our horrific human gestures, act out desires to the full, cutting their way to their final goal through their predestined obstacles [...] We are in the presence of a prodigious example of humour, cruelty and innocence fused in one flesh, and along with them a tight sequence of chance events. We have the impression we are witnessing truth being turned inside out, truth being skinned alive.

In an article extensively reproduced by Dalí in *The Secret Life of Salvador Dalí* (1968: 212), Eugenio Montes, a fellow-student of Buñuel and Dalí at the Residencia de Estudiantes and a writer, links the film to the violence of Spanish culture:

> Barbarous, elementary beauty, the moon and the earth of the desert, where 'blood is sweeter than honey', reappear before the world. No! No! Do not look for the roses of France. Spain is not a garden, nor the Spaniard a gardener. Spain is a planet and the roses of the desert are rotten donkeys. Hence no wit, no decorativism. The Spaniard is essence, not refinement. Spain does not refine, it cannot falsify. Spain cannot paint turtles or disguise donkeys with

> crystals instead of their skin. The sculptured Christs in Spain bleed, and when they are brought out into the streets they march between two rows of Civil Guards. (Montes 1929)[11]

The rhetorical excesses of such comments indicate an enthusiastic poetic response to the excesses of the film rather than a measured critical assessment. Cyril Connolly, writing in 1934, reacts in a similarly dithyrambic mode:

> This contemptuous private world of jealousy and lust, of passion and aridity, whose beautiful occupants patter about like stoats in search of blood, produced an indescribable effect, a tremendous feeling of excitement and liberation. The Id has spoken and – through the obsolete medium of silent film – the spectators had been treated to their first glimpses of despair and frenzy which were smouldering beneath the complacent post-war world [...] With the impression of having witnessed some infinitely ancient horror, Saturn swallowing his sons, we made our way out into the cold of February (sic) 1929, that unique and dazzling cold. (quoted in Baxter 1994: 93)

Connolly describes how the film was received with boos, and states that hats and sticks were thrown at the screen, while a woman shouted: 'Salopes, salopes, salopes!' / 'Bitches!'. He was clearly confusing *Un chien andalou* with the stormy reception of *L'Age d'or* the following year.

Other reactions were more muted, if not hostile, as testified for example in the critical review of *La Revue du cinéma* (1929). Although this journal had published the script in June 1929, it was less than enthusiastic about the film in its November issue. Its reviewer reproaches critics of the film for 'selling old stock of quite indigestible psychoanalytical jargon', and quotes Alexandre Arnoux (writing on the film for the *Nouvelles littéraires*): 'I assure you the film is fashionable Freudian matter. Repression, an endless outpouring of aborted acts, sexual perversion, libido, transfer and complexes.' The review also cites Jean Vincent Bréchignac (reviewing the film for the popular film journal *Pour vous*), who patronizingly dismisses the film as an adolescent prank: 'What could be more engaging than a young man carried away by his enthusiasm or a burst of passing rebellion?' Other reviewers were less than enthusiastic about the film. The philosopher Raymond Aron (1929) contrasts the films of Buster Keaton, which subvert social conventions from within, with Man Ray's *Mystère du château du Dé* and *Un chien andalou*, which he claims are situated in a void, outside social norms. He concludes that Keaton's revolt is more 'fecund' than the 'witticism and harmless onanism' of Man Ray or Buñuel. For J. Bouissounouse (1929), writing in *La Revue du cinéma*, the film was quite incomprehensible, 'absurd from beginning to end', and notes that the hysterical laughter of the women in the audience was matched by the boredom of male spectators. And a final example: in a particularly scathing review of the film published in the popular journal *Nouvel Age*, Edouard Peisson (1931), while conceding that the image of the slashed eye is indeed beautiful, states that 'it is also stupid and morbid, fit for the audience of a Punch and Judy show'. He concludes that if the great majority of spectators miss the main point, it's because the film is of interest to a few idle people who see themselves as intellectuals![12]

This cross-section of critical responses leads one to conclude that Dalí's claim regarding the impact of the film might well have been exaggerated, and that the film aquired its radical aura retrospectively. The surrealists accepted the scandal and rejected the success. They enthusiastically supported the film, which was immediately appropriated as a model of, and for, Surrealism. In a review published on 28 June 1929 in *Le Merle*, for instance, the surrealist Robert Desnos focuses on the impact of the eye-slitting scene, noting the film's mix of poetry and humour, essential ingredients of surrealist works:

> I do not know any film that affects the spectator so directly, and is made so specifically for him, engaging him in conversation, in an intimate rapport. But whether it's the eye sliced by a razor, whose crystalline liquid trickles viscously, or the assemblage of Spanish priests and grand pianos bearing its load of dead donkeys, there is nothing in it that does not draw on humour and poetry, which are intimately linked. (Desnos 1992: 187)

In his review of the film, the surrealist Jacques Brunius (1929: 230–1) compares the logic of the narrative to the 'absurd and implacable necessity of dreams' and claims that its association of ideas and images corresponds to surrealist automatism. He contrasts the purely technical acrobatics of 'pure cinema' (he is referring to 1920s avant-garde film) with the importance of the script in *Un chien andalou*. He imagines the opening scene as an assault on the complacent bourgeois aesthete: 'In the first minute of the film with a slash of his razor Buñuel rams back into their sockets the shining eyes of seekers of pretty shots, aesthetes, those easily offended by what they see. There can be no misunderstanding, the rest of the film is totally lacking in harmony'. Brunius predicted, however, that the film would be appropriated by the cultured public: 'For those who are familiar with the habits of specialist cinemas and avant-garde spectators, who adore being violated, it is easy to predict for Buñuel a fine *succès de scandale*'. The film was indeed adopted by the cultured public, and was very soon the talk of fashionable salons. For communist film critic Léon Moussinac (1929), for example, the film expresses modish sadism, 'a decadent distraction of poor taste', rather than a critique of the bourgeoisie.

To counter the film's recuperation the surrealists reacted by elaborating a type of celebratory poetic criticism, as in this later overview of Buñuel's cinema by Benjamin Péret (1952: 27–8):

> For the first time, cinema, disdaining vain anecdote, tried to plunge into the abyss of the human soul in order to bring back to the surface the grimacing beasts that lead a life of caged lions about to devour their keeper. The spectator could only be irritated by this film which, coming from the depths, reveals to him what he stubbornly hid from himself. He suddenly felt naked in his own eyes and in the eyes of others, ready to see himself as he is, stripped of the fine sentiments he liked decking himself out in.

The poet thus mimics in his text the irrationality and excesses of the film. Such a poetic reading focuses on the effect of the film on the viewer rather than on its meaning. It is a subjective response largely internal to Surrealism, which elects to preserve the enigmatic qualities and poetic aura of the film by imitating its style, thereby displaying a refusal to retrieve the film through rational discourse. Creative misreadings also belong to this category of response to the film. For example, Oswell Blakeston (1929) reports that the female protagonist puts on lipstick while ants swarm out of the man's mouth; while the composer George Antheil puts together his own personal montage, several years after seeing the film:

> [...] The young man with the razor pursues the girl, who, as she runs from room to room in a building with apparently endless rooms in it, has her clothes alternately dissolve and materialise as she runs along. One moment she is nude. The next moment she is clothed. And so on, clothes, nudity, clothes, nudity, clothes. She runs through one room to the next, closing doors all the while. Sometimes the fellow gets his hands caught in the closing doors, and one sees a close-up of a clenched fist apparently decaying, with ants running all over it. None of this stops him, however; he keeps on going. The going gets harder twoards the end. The girl comes to the last room and is huddling, nude,

> in the furthest corner of the room while the fellow strains towards her with two big cables attached to his shoulders. (1945: 301)

Following the screening of the film, Dalí and Buñuel were enthusiastically adopted by the surrealist group. However, there are conflicting accounts of their first meetings with the group. Buñuel first met Louis Aragon and Man Ray, but was he introduced by Christian Zervos or the artist Fernand Léger? Was the first meeting at the café La Coupole or Le Dôme? Did Buñuel meet the surrealist group at the café Cyrano on Place Pigalle before the opening night of the film? Did André Breton, leader of the surrealist group, summon Buñuel and Dalí to the café Radio in Boulevard Clichy, after seeing the film at Studio 28 in October? Whatever the facts of their first encounter with the group, the film effectively opened the door to Surrealism for Dalí and Buñuel. After the première, they attended the surrealists' daily meetings at the Cyrano or at Breton's studio. As Georges Sadoul (1965: 19) recalls: 'Buñuel didn't need to say much for us to understand he was one of us [...] He belonged body and soul to our group even before having met any one of us'.

Yet they had to cross Breton's hurdles before being fully accepted as surrealists. The main initiation was linked to the incident of the publication of the screenplay (Buñuel 1984: 108–10). Paul Eluard invited Buñuel to publish it in a special number on Surrealism of the Belgian journal *Variétés*, but it had already been promised to *La Revue du cinéma*, which belonged to the publisher Gallimard. Summoned by Breton to an inquisitorial meeting attended by the entire surrealist group, Buñuel was accused of collaborating in a bourgeois publication and producing a commercially successful film. 'How could such a scandalous film draw such an enormous public?' asked Aragon in his role as prosecutor, while Breton asked bluntly: 'The question is, are you with the police or with us?' Although Buñuel and Eluard were sent with hammers to the Gallimard printworks to smash up the type, the issue had already been printed. Letters of protest against Gallimard were sent to several Paris newspapers. Buñuel, it seems, was even prepared to ritualistically burn the negative on the place du Tertre in Montmartre!

By the end of 1929 Buñuel and Dalí were fully integrated into the surrealist group. Breton's enthusiastic preface to Dalí's first Paris exhibition, held in November 1929 at the Galerie Goemans, gives the works the stamp of surrealist authenticity, focusing on their link to the unconscious and their hallucinatory qualities. The December issue of *La Révolution surréaliste* reproduced two of the paintings exhibited, *Illuminated Pleasures* and *The Accommodation of Desires* (which had been bought by Breton). It also reproduced a photomontage by Magritte of photobooth portraits of the entire surrealist group, including Buñuel and Dalí, eyes closed, framing the painting of a female nude figure by Magritte. The same issue published the script of *Un chien andalou*, with a short preface by Buñuel, expressing his passionate and unconditional allegiance to Surrealism:

> The publication of this screenplay in *La Révolution surréaliste is the only one I authorize.* It expresses unconditionally my complete identification with surrealist thought and activity. *Un chien andalou* would not exist if Surrealism did not exist.
>
> 'A successful film', that's what most of the people who have seen it think. But what can I do against those who adore novelty, even when novelty offends their deepest convictions, against a corrupt or insincere press, against that pack of imbeciles who finds *beautiful* and *poetic* what, in reality, is nothing less than a desperate, passionate call to murder. (Buñuel 1929)

Buñuel aligns himself with the surrealists when he describes the film not in aesthetic terms as *beautiful* or *poetic* – an allusion to the predominantly aesthetic qualities of avant-garde films – but as an anarchist gesture. By claiming that the film was a 'desperate, passionate call to murder' he sought to allay the surrealists' fears of its recuperation by the bourgeoisie, 'that pack of imbeciles' – although, ironically, his text takes up the very words used on the commercial poster for the Studio 28 screening of the film: 'Ce film est un appel au meurtre'! His text echoes Breton's statement in his *Second Manifesto of Surrealism*, published in the same issue of the journal: 'The simplest surrealist act consists of dashing down into the street, pistol in hand, and firing blindly, as fast as you can pull the trigger, into the crowd' (Breton 1972: 125). Dalí had already published a similar declaration in *Mirador* (24 October 1929), where he also rejected the success of the film, defending its irrecuperable violence:

> *Un chien andalou* had an unprecedented success in Paris; which provokes our indignation just like any other public success would. But we think that the audience which applauded *Un chien andalou* is an audience stupefied by

avant-garde magazines and 'divulgences', an audience which applauds everything new and bizarre out of snobbery. This public did not understand the moral basis of the film which is aimed directly at it with total violence and cruelty. (Dalí 1998: 109)

Buñuel and Dalí were both active in the group in the early 1930s. They contributed texts to *Le Surréalisme au service de la révolution* (1930–33), which replaced *La Révolution surréaliste*. Max Ernst's 1931 photomontage of the surrealists, *Au rendez-vous des amis or Loplop Introduces the surrealist group*, reproduced in the fourth issue of the journal (1931), includes photographs of Dalí and Buñuel pasted over a display of knives, while a gigantic eyeball appears to the right of the two figures. Dalí worked on a scenario for a documentary on Surrealism, which was never made (Radford 1997: 102), and produced a frontispiece for Breton's *Second Manifesto of Surrealism* (June 1930). Breton would later recall that Dalí embodied the surrealist spirit at that time. The collaboration with the surrealist movement was, however, shortlived. By 1936, Dalí was excluded from the group for his support of Franco in the Spanish Civil War (against the Republican cause defended by the surrealists), as well as for the commercial exploitation of his art (which earned him the label 'Avida Dollars', an anagramme of his name). The fascist, monarchist and catholic Dalí no longer had anything in common with the leftwing ideals of the surrealist group. As for Buñuel, although he left the surrealist movement in 1932, he continued to identify with its principles, as testified in the importance of dream and the unconscious in his films. Many years later, in his memoirs, he noted the profound effect of Surrealism on his later work:

I treasure that access to the depths of the self which I so yearned for, that call to the irrational, to the impulses that spring from the dark side of the soul. It was the surrealists who first launched this appeal with a sustained force and courage, with insolence and playfulness and an obstinate dedication to fight everything repressive in conventional wisdom. (Buñuel 1984: 123)

Dalí and Buñuel both continued to promote scandal and revolution, principles which were at the core of surrealist theory and practice. As Buñuel (1984:107) writes about their participation in Surrealism:

All of us were supporters of a certain concept of revolution, and although the surrealists didn't consider themselves terrorists, they were constantly fighting a society they despised. Their principal weapon wasn't guns, of course: it was scandal. Scandal was a potent agent of revelation, capable of exposing such

> social crimes as the exploitation of one man by another, colonialist imperialism, religious tyranny – in sum, all the secret and odious underpinnings of a system that had to be destroyed. The real purpose of Surrealism was not to create a new literary, artistic, or even philosophical movement, but to explode the social order, to transform life itself.

They continued to refer to the film as quintessentially surrealist, in other words scandalous and revolutionary. The scandal lay above all in the moral 'passionate call to murder' enacted in the prologue, which corresponded to the surrealists' glorification of the unmotivated crime. When it was first screened in Studio 28, Buñuel is reported to have said that 'People fainted, there was an abortion, and more than thirty denunciations to the police' (Turrent and Colina 1993: 34). For Dalí also the aim was to provoke, scandalize and assault: '*Le Chien andalou* was the film of adolescence and death which I was going to plunge right into the heart of witty, elegant and intellectualized Paris with all the reality and all the weight of the Iberian dagger' (Dalí 1968: 212). The composer George Antheil (1945: 301) recalls a private screening of the film in Hollywood in 1937:

> Cecil B. DeMille, king of the surrealists (American branch), was a pale green when the lights went up. He got up and left without a word.
> So did the others, when they recovered.
> Dalí ran out to a phone immediately. He called his wife, Gala. 'Gala,' he said breathlessly, 'it was the *greatest* success imaginable. They were *speechless!*'

Likewise, in his introduction to the screening of the film in Madrid in 1929 Buñuel declared: 'I don't want the film to please you but to offend you. I would be sorry if you enjoyed it' (Aranda 1975: 64). Later, in 1947, he asserted that the aim of the film was 'to provoke in the spectator instinctive reactions of attraction and of repulsion' (Mellen 1978: 151). In 'The Cinema, instrument of poetry' (1958), he refers to the cinema as 'a marvelous and dangerous weapon if a free spirit wields it'. Paraphrasing the words of Octavio Paz he declares that 'it would suffice for the white eyelid of the screen to reflect the light proper to it to blow up the universe' (Hammond 2000: 114, 112).

## A surrealist film?

Buñuel's enthusiasm for the cinema was shared, at least during the years of the silent cinema, by the surrealists themselves. The cinema was central to the surrealists, who were film-goers first and foremost, and script writers, film reviewers and film-makers only in second place.[13] Their childhood coincided with the invention of cinema – Breton was born in 1896, the year of the Lumière brothers' first films – and their adolescence with the highly popular serials such as Louis Feuillade's crime thrillers *Fantômas* (1913–14) and *Les Vampires* (1915–16) with their mix of violence, eroticism and unmotivated crimes.[14] They saw in mass culture, and the silent cinema in particular, a new revolutionary language capable of expressing both social revolt and sexual fantasies. Cinema was linked to the modernist aesthetic: 'it is there that the only *absolutely modern* mystery is celebrated', writes Breton (Hammond 2000: 74). His position is echoed by Dalí, who declares: 'Modernity does not mean the canvases painted by Sonia Delaunay, nor Fritz Lang's *Metropolis*, but hockey sweaters manufactured anonymously in England; it means B-grade movies with the world's oldest jokes which make you laugh' (Dalí 1998: 44–5). He lists film as an example of modernity alongside gin cocktails and sports cars, boxing, electric light, jazz and the gramophone!

The surrealists rejected the formal experimentation of 1920s' avant-garde films in favour of a form of cinema allegedly free from a stylistic tradition. They admired horror films such as Robert Wiene's *Das Kabinett des Dr Caligari* (1919), American comedy (Chaplin, Keaton, Langdon, Sennett) and romantic melodrama (Hathaway's 1935 film *Peter Ibbetson* was considered by Breton 'a triumph of surrealist thought'). The very absence of artistry in films enhanced for the surrealists their lyrical qualities. Thus Desnos (1922: 111) expresses his passion for Murnau's *Nosferatu* (1922), 'where no innovation was arbitrary, and all was sacrificed to poetry and nothing to art'. *Un chien andalou*, with its few technical effects, clearly shares with these films a simplicity and disdain for technical virtuosity.

The surrealists were fascinated by the surreal qualities of commercial films, not so much as a storytelling medium (they rejected literary qualities in film and painting) but for the power of the cinematic image to fascinate, shock, and create the marvelous out of the real. Above all, the surrealists appreciated the film medium because it creates an illusory space, abolishing the spatio-temporal laws which order reality. Hence it is a privileged means for the expression of desires and dreams, as Philippe Soupault recalled with enthusiasm:

> The cinema was for us a great discovery in the early days of Surrealism [...] At that time we considered film as a marvellous means for expressing dreams. We thought that film would offer extraordinary possibilities for expressing, transfiguring and realizing dreams. For me, film, even more than literature or theatre, conferred on men a superior power. *Everything was permitted in the cinema*. (Mabire 1965: 29)

Surrealists saw the 'salles obscures' of cinema as a space conducive to the creation of the surreal defined as a transformation of the real. As Michel Leiris states: 'In order to have surrealism, you must first have realism, you must have a reality to manipulate' (Leiris 1992: 16). For Dalí film has the potential to transform the raw material of reality: 'The tree, the street, the rugby match, are transsubstantiated in a disturbing way in film' (Dalí 1998: 23). As a result, in film, as in Surrealism in general, 'the real and the imagined, past and future [...] cease to be perceived as contradictions' (Breton 1972: 123), they have the same ontological reality, combining fantasy and everyday reality seamlessly.

Surrealist viewing practices promoted the active engagement of the viewer's imagination. In 'As in a Wood' (1951), Breton's celebration of the silent cinema, he recalled the times when, in wartime Nantes, he would enter a cinema at random with fellow dadaist Jacques Vaché, view a sequence or two – sometimes opening cans, cutting up bread and uncorking bottles, all the while conversing loudly as if at table! – then leave, repeating the process in another cinema. Refusing predictable storylines they would assemble the sequences into an incongruous montage which they found *magnetizing* (Hammond 2000: 73–5). The cinema was thus for the surrealists analogous to the space of the Paris streets or the flea-market, a site of chance encounters with objects or images taken out of their original context and refashioned and collaged in line with their fantasies.

However passionate the surrealists were about the silent cinema, their enthusiasm waned with the arrival of the talkies. Their disappointment was expressed in the group's 'Manifesto of the surrealists concerning *L'Age d'or*', published for the launch of the film in 1930, where they stated that only a few fragments could be salvaged from the mediocre production of the contemporary cinema. In spite of the surrealists' fascination for the film medium and their important contribution to film discourse of the 1920s, they actually produced many scenarios (Artaud, Desnos, Péret) but few films. Their own listings varied over the years, in relation to ideological disputes and shifting political agendas. The *Dictionnaire abrégé du surréalisme / Short Dictionary of Surrealism* (1938) lists Man Ray's *Emak Bakia* (1926) and *L'Etoile de mer* (1928), Duchamp's *Anemic cinema* (1925), Hugnet's *La Perle* (1929) as well as *Un chien andalou* and *L'Age d'or*.

*Un chien andalou* was enthusiastically received at a time when the first 'heroic' phase of Surrealism – and the silent cinema – were coming to an end. Breton had evicted a number of the early members from the movement, which was in need of renewal. For the surrealist group *Un chien andalou* was a revolutionary film, insofar as it sought to destroy oppressive bourgeois institutions – politics, marriage, religion, art, morality. It was seen by them as a transgressive film, hence liberatory. For Desnos, '[o]nly candour is revolutionary [...] It's this candour that enables us today to equate the real revolutionary films, *Potemkin, The Gold Rush, The Wedding March* and *Un chien andalou*' (Hammond 1978: 37).

Yet, in spite of Buñuel and Dalí's enthusiastic peddling of the film as surrealist, and the surrealists' own passionate and poetic appropriation of the film, is this a surrealist film? It is true that *Un chien andalou* appears to have been cast in a deliberately surrealist mould, and can be considered surrealist for its alleged automatism and free association, its dreamlike elements, its violent images, its radical montage structure, its assault on the spectator. 'In many ways *Un chien andalou* is André Breton's *Manifeste du surréalisme* put into practice', claim one critic (Edwards 2004: 143). Moreover, although Buñuel later maintained that the film, unlike *L'Age d'or*, does not contain any social critique, the film can also be read as an indictment of oppressive bourgeois institutions, in keeping with Surrealism's revolutionary aim, inherited from Marx and Rimbaud, to 'transform the world' and 'change life'. Its symbols of repression and inhibition (pianos and Marists, the policeman reprimanding the androgyne, the B-cop dad reprimanding his son, stultifying bourgeois marriage) testify to its impact as a powerful social drama (see chapter 3). Denise Tual considers it 'a piercing cry never heard before, which sounds the death knoll of certain bourgeois beliefs' (Tual 1978: 104). But what exactly is a surrealist film? Certainly *Un chien andalou* is quite unlike Man Ray's or Duchamp's films, and seems to share features with American comedy films (Langdon, Sennett, Keaton) which, according to the surrealists, have 'surreal' qualities. It could equally well be considered a dada film for its non-narrative elements, disjunctive images, playful montage and irreverential parodies. Alternately – apart from the prologue which could be bracketed off as a dream or fantasy sequence – it could be considered as a realistic film (contrasting with the abstraction of avant-garde cinema).

'There is no surrealist painting', declared Pierre Naville in 1925, contending that there is no single pictorial style in Surrealism. Similarly, in 1929 there was no one model for surrealist film and subsequent 'surrealist' films were too diverse to fit into one style. Indeed, the surrealists did not privilege the film medium above painting, poetry or photography. In fact they expressed a cavalier indifference, even disdain, for the filmic medium – as they did for painting, 'that lamentable expedient'. The cinema, like painting or poetry, was simply a means to create the surreal.

*Un chien andalou* did not fit the canon; it produced it. Within Surrealism itself, however, it was to function less as a model for making further surrealist films than as a yardstick for assessing the violence and sadism of other surrealist works. For example, Georges Bataille (1985: 28) interprets Dalí's paintings through the lens of the opening images of the film: 'Dalí's razors carve into our faces the grimaces of horror that probably risk making us vomit like drunkards this servile nobility, this idiotic idealism that leaves us under the spell of a few comical prison bosses'. His reading of the paintings is filtered through the film's violent imagery as well as de Sade's images of mutilation and violence. The surrealist Georges Hugnet (1931: 338) also alludes to the film when writing about Miró's 1930 paintings:

> We find once again a Spanish legacy of cruelty, insolence and pride, in this taste for blood and atrocious symbolic realism. There is also 'a desperate call to murder' in these torture instruments for the new Inquisition. Art at the foot of the fetish, at the foot of taboos, is carrying the rope, is pierced by nails, strangled and crucified by material images. Dalí's sadism has its own torture chamber.

The shared imagery of Miró's paintings and *Un chien andalou* – realism and symbolism combined, fetish and taboo images, the rope, the pierced hands, symbols of the Catholic church – is fused in Hugnet's text with an hallucinatory vision of the Spanish Inquisition. These references suggest that the example of *Un chien andalou* provided a model which helped formulate comments on other limit-forms of expression, such as the violent images of the unconscious in Dalí and Miró's paintings.

However, to reduce the import of this film to an account of the directors' intentions or the (conflicting) myths of its production, to the enthusiastic or scandalized reception of its viewers or its recuperation by the bourgeois public, to an illustration of surrealist theory or an exemplar of surrealist practice, would be to foreclose the complexity of reactions and meanings produced by the film. Once it entered the public domain, the film gave rise to a complex network of diverse and often divergent comments and interpretations. It is this complexity and diversity which will be explored in the following chapters.

## Notes

1 For production details see Aranda (1975), Conrad (1976), Buñuel (1984), Talens (1993), Baxter (1994), Drummond (1994). For the collaboration between Buñuel and Dalí see Sánchez Vidal (1994), Finkelstein (1996).
2 See also Turrent (1992: 30), Aub (1991: 51).
3 The original typescript, titled 'Vaya Marista!', was published by Alfonso Puyal (1999).
4 See also Aub (1991: 48– 9).
5 For shooting details see Baxter (1994).
6 When the money provided by Buñuel's mother ran out, a rich Spaniard, Ricardo Soriano, seems to have provided more funding (Tual 1987: 100–1).
7 The film is usually shown at 24 frames per second. However, silent films were normally shot at 16 frames per second. Ferrán Alberich's recent restored version (Filmoteca Española 2003) is 24 minutes long.
8 See for example Drouzy (1978: 40–1), Edwards (1982: 56).
9 A large number of critics mistakenly state the film was first shown in 1928.

10 The producer and theatre-director Pierre Braunberger bought the theatrical rights to the film for his company Studio-Film (Baxter 1994: 88).
11 See chapter 3 for a discussion of references to Spanish culture in the film.
12 Other reviews of the film after its first screening include: (in Paris) Comtesse de Beaumont (1929), Ghéon (1929), Lenauer (1929); (in Barcelona) Artigas (1929), Masoliver (1929), Piqueras (1929); (in London) Blakeston (1929).
13 For studies of Surrealism and the cinema see Kyrou (1963), Matthews (1971), Short (2002), Richardson (2006).
14 On the importance of Fantômas for the surrealists, see Walz (2000), Eburne (2008).

# 2 Romantic melodrama or magic theatre?

Let's kill the moonlight!
Filippo Marinetti

A moonlit night, a violent crime, the complicity between torturer and victim, male seduction and female resistance, frustrated sexual chases, murder, separation, and death: *Un chien andalou* contains narrative elements familiar to spectators of silent cinema's romantic dramas. For Dalí the poetry of film lies precisely in the stock images of popular melodrama, 'the villain's mask, his movements, his manner of dressing, a hand knocking at the door' (Dalí 1998: 40). Yet the coherent unfolding of a storyline is constantly impeded by apparently random images, visual tricks and gags, elements that disrupt and displace the narrative and disorient the viewer. This chapter explores the ways in which *Un chien andalou* both adopts and rejects cinematic storytelling conventions. Are we in the presence of a main narrative, shot through and destabilized by extraneous elements? Or is the film constructed as a collage, with distinct temporalities and part-narratives, as an assemblage of disparate scenes that do not make up a coherent whole? While a number of critics have integrated the apparently disjunctive elements into an overarching narrative, notably through psychological or psychoanalytical interpretations, this chapter will argue that the film is made up of two distinct, heterogeneous temporalities, and that narrative and non-narrative elements are in a dialectic relation, held in tension and resisting integration into a single storyline or a totalizing interpretation.

## Classic film narrative subverted

*Un chien andalou* both adopts and subverts the narrative conventions of 1920s' cinema. As a drama of passions, the excessive actions (the violence of the initial crime, the herculean struggle between man and pianos, the theatricality of the seduction scene, the morbidity of the couple buried in the sand), exaggerated gestures (the script refers to the main protagonist 'looking like a villain in a melodrama') and heightened emotions (lust, romance, terror) recall the theatrical genre of melodrama. However, whereas classic melodrama unfolds in a linear way, from the suspense of enigma to the closure of solution – the mystery is solved and order is finally restored – this is not the case in the script and film of *Un chien andalou*, where the melodramatic framework is adapted and perverted to playful ends. The story has (at least) two beginnings, several (absurd) digressions, and three (inconclusive) endings. Its female protagonist appears to have miraculously survived an earlier disfigurement, while its male protagonist is doubled, dies and resuscitates. As for temporality, it combines the fictional time of the fairytale, a precise yet jumbled chronological development, and the immediacy of fragmented images. The following section explores these aspects of the film in more detail.

### *Plot structure*

The story appears to have two beginnings – the eye-slitting scene and the sequence of the cyclist riding down a Paris street – yet the relation between the two remains unexplained. Indeed the prologue itself appears as a separate, self-enclosed narrative. It takes place in an imaginary time, the horrific crime has no visible consequences, and the criminal, like Fantômas the 'Emperor of crime', exits the story once his act has been accomplished. The unfolding of a coherent storyline appears to be halted by further digressions, such as the sequence with the androgyne and the severed hand, and the death of the double. Moreover, extraneous elements – or fragments from a second narrative interrupting the first? – impede the coherent progression of the narrative: scenes such as the hand swarming with ants, the transformation of ants to a woman's armpit hair to a sea-urchin. Dramatic development is also arrested by three partial or false closures: the successful accomplishment of the eye-slitting crime, the death of the androgyne and the death of the hero's double. Even the 'final' ending does not bring closure and is itself inexplicable, contradicting the romantic nature of the couple's walk along the beach, and leaving the mystery of the original act unsolved.

*Characterization*

Characters themselves are nameless and, with their inconsistent behaviour and uncertain identities, fail to fulfil the role of narrative anchor. The eye-slashing criminal – played by Buñuel himself, whose name does not appear in the credits – wears a watch when sharpening his razor, yet when slashing the eye he is watchless but has acquired a striped tie. He vanishes from the scene, his violent act left unexplained and unpunished. His victim – or accomplice? – loses an eye, yet reappears 'eight years later' with both eyes miraculously intact. Her role shifts in the course of the action from maternal to sexual, passive to active, object to subject. She later undergoes Batcheff's caresses which jumble her breasts and buttocks, survives the exchange of body parts with Batcheff, and walks calmly onto the beach. The principal male protagonist has several roles: cyclist (not overly skilful), seducer (not entirely successful) and double (feared then killed) – and possibly the man buried in the sand in the final freeze frame. He appears to have magical powers (he can turn breasts into buttocks, books into guns). His behaviour is erratic: as a cyclist he hovers between child and adult, male and female; his actions are docile (he lies passively on the bed) and desperate (he drags an impossible load); his sexual identity is unfixed when he exchanges body parts with Mareuil; the limits of his body are dissolved when ants swarm out of a hole in his hand, his mouth is erased, and his face is invaded by female body hair. Instability and randomness also characterize minor characters. One of the priests dragged along by Batcheff is played in one shot by Dalí and replaced in the following shot by Jaime Miravilles. The youth (male or female?) clutches a diagonal box (belonging to the cyclist?) with a severed hand (whose hand?) and lets him- / herself get run over by a passing car (why?). The young man on the beach (played by Robert Hommet), who is joined by Mareuil when she leaves Batcheff, appears from nowhere, and is almost immediately half-buried in the sand – or is this Batcheff's fate? As a consequence of the tenuous psychological substance of the characters, interest is constantly displaced to the dramatic function and physical presence of objects such as the razor, the box or the tie.

*Time and space*

The logic of realist narrative is also undermined by temporal and spatial inconsistencies throughout the film, both profilmic (non-media specific) and filmic (through montage). Temporally, the film combines the timelessness of the fairytale ('Once upon a time'), the (more-or-less) linear development of the principal storyline, and the immediacy of isolated shots or sequences. The intertitles, a key feature of silent cinema, whose role was to anchor the narrative and orient the spectator, function here as mock announcements of a classic five-act story, presenting precise yet jumbled temporal markers. The opening intertitle, 'Once upon a time', situates the narrative in the suspended time of fairytales. The precise temporal indication 'Eight years later' contradicts the timelessness of the fairytale narrative, and appears totally arbitrary. 'Towards three in the morning' is also both overprecise and unmotivated. 'Sixteen years before' suggests a flashback, yet the following shot presents the same actors and location and a continuation of the same action. The final intertitle, 'In the spring', promises renewal but introduces a freeze frame of disintegration and death.

Spatial inconsistencies also disrupt the realistic unfolding of the story. For example, the window at which Buñuel sharpens his razor has curtains, yet is curtainless when he steps out onto the balcony. The window gives first onto a balcony, then onto a quiet street, and finally onto a busy thoroughfare. The furniture in the apartment room changes place several times. The door in the apartment leads first into an identical room, then onto a landing, and finally directly onto the beach. Such inconsistencies have the effect of destabilizing any sense of spatial coherence and literally

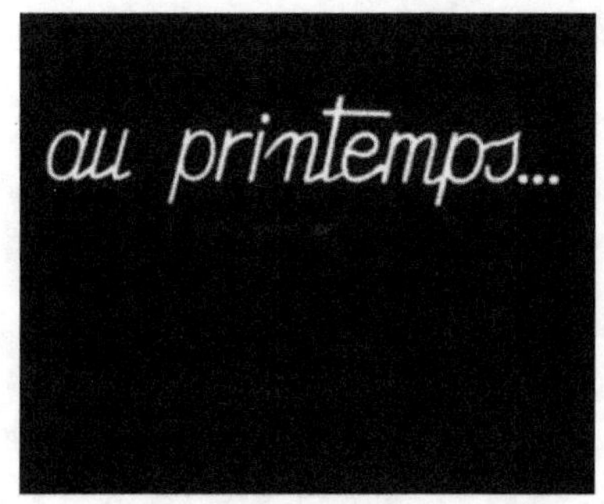


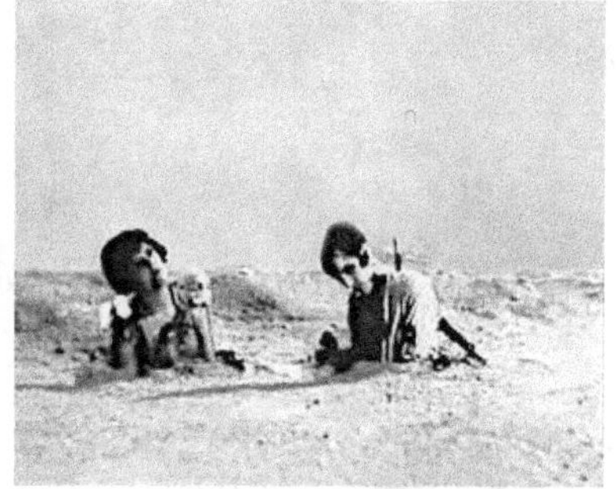

In the springtime…

disorienting the spectator. Moreover, spatial uncertainties are compounded by the uncertain location of objects or actions. For example, in what diegetic space and time can we situate the sea-urchin, the cocktail-shaker, the desert location at the end? How can a single apartment room hold two grand pianos, donkeys and priests? Does the death-moth sequence belong to the realist narrative or to a fantasy sequence? Such ambiguities serve to further disrupt narrative logic.

*Editing*

Continuity editing, which establishes logical spatial and temporal links between shots, conventionally creates the illusion of narrative coherence and progression. The film-makers use standard continuity editing as in classic film realism – match-cuts on action, eyeline matches, shot-reverse-shot – which ensures smooth links between the shots, thereby naturalizing the action. Yet within the classic montage framework minor spatio-temporal inconsistencies are introduced. Continuity of action is sometimes matched with spatial discontinuity to undermine realism and destabilize fixed spatial references. For example, when the male protagonist's double is killed, he falls in the room, then through a dissolve continues his fall in a park. The undermining of seamless editing and spatial congruence is also a consequence of eyeline (mis)matches: the female protagonist's gaze through the apartment window first situates the cyclist on the same level as the apartment window, while the couple later

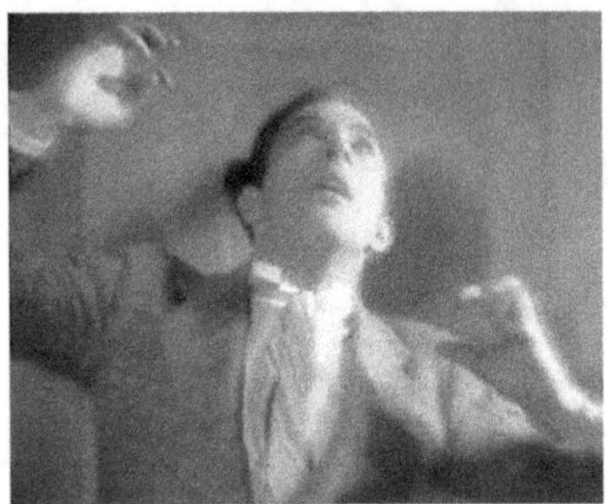

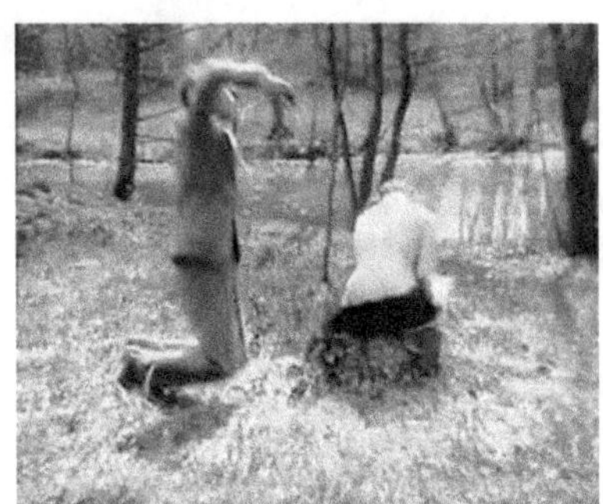

Falling from room to park

looks down from the window onto the street (Drummond 1994: xxii). These examples lead one to conclude that, rather than rejecting cinematic illusion, Buñuel plays with it, using continuity editing to skew continuity in space and time, perverting classic codes of editing from within. As in avant-garde films – or an amateur movie – the film is full of minor inconsistencies that subtly undermine the seamlessness of classic editing, foregrounding the montage process itself.

*Soundtrack*

The soundtrack, alternating Wagner's *Liebestod* from his opera *Tristan und Isolde* with two Argentinian tangos, is structured like a musical collage which seems to have its own dynamics independent of the narrative. Entirely extra-diegetic, the music alternately accompanies and contradicts the action. The Wagner sequences, accompanying the scenes of love (seduction), death (of the androgyne and the double), and the death of love (death-head moth sequence), heighten the emotional charge of the narrative; while the tangos, which accompany the eye-slitting scene, the seduction scene and the ending, contradict these scenes of violence with their light-heartedness.

Not only is the plot disrupted or undermined by non-sequiturs that impede or arrest the unfolding of the story from within, it is also juxtaposed with sequences that appear to run parallel with, or counter to, the main narrative, and seem difficult to integrate into the storyline. On the contrary, these counter-narrative elements compete with and displace the main narrative.

*Repetition and serialization*

Firstly, narrative progression is countered by elements of repetition and serialization. On the level of the action, there is repetition for example when the woman walks out of the room into an identical room, where the cyclist is lying on a bed in a similar position. On the thematic level, examples of repetition include the leitmotifs of the tie (which migrates from criminal's neck to cyclist's box to bed to beach), the box (which moves from cyclist to androgyne, and from bed to beach again), the ants (shown twice emerging from a hole in the hero's hand), severed hands (the criminal's razor-wielding hand, the ant-infested hand caught in the door, the hand in the street prodded by the androgyne's stick then placed in the box). Further, circular or diagonal shapes are serialized, as in the following sequence, quoted from the screenplay:

> Close-up of the hand full of ants crawling out of a black hole in the palm. None of the ants fall off.
> Dissolve to the hairs on the armpit of a young woman who is lying on a beach in the sunshine. Dissolve to the undulating spines of a sea-urchin. Dissolve to the head of a girl seen directly from above. This shot is taken as though through the iris of an eye: the iris opens to reveal a group of people standing around the girl [...]

The entire series is linked by the formal repetition of circular shapes. Repetition and serialization are examples of associative play, which impede or displace diegetic development by introducing circular or lateral associations (as in Benjamin Péret's poetry, much admired by Buñuel and Dalí). Rather than matches on action which ensure a coherent narrative development between shots, graphic matches dominate in these associations, linking the images formally rather than diegetically, through cuts (moon to eye) or dissolves (body hair to sea-urchin), suggesting a poetic structure in which visual rhyming conflicts with the development of a linear narrative. Narrative cohesion is thus displaced by the purely formal. Unlike conventional narrative structures, where space and time are subordinated to the logic of causality, these associative structures are dominated by poetic rhetoric and the logic of the imagination. These shifts between narrative and poetic logic are suggested in Jean Vigo's (1930) description of the film as 'primarily a subjective drama fashioned into a poem'. The film thus has affinities with avant-garde films of the 1920s, such as Man Ray's *L'Etoile de mer* (1928), which is elaborated through the repetition and association of images, suggesting a poetic rather than a narrative structure. *Un chien andalou* differs from the avant-garde cinema, however, insofar as its narrative elements also link it to 1920s' mainstream cinema (see chapter 3 for a discussion of the parodic use of cinematic genres).

*Close-up shots*

Another instance of filmic strategies that compete with the development of the narrative is the large number of striking close-ups, which include the slashed eye, the severed hand, the hand with ants, the armpit hair, the death-head moth. Both Dalí and Buñuel were fascinated by the close-up in film and photography. For Buñuel, cinematic art originated with Griffith's first use of the close-up in 1913. The last issue of *L'Amic de les Arts* (March 1929), co-edited by Dalí, includes the reproduction of a photograph by Moholy-Nagy (from *Painting, Photography, Film* 1927) of the close-up of the eye of a marabou, with the caption: 'There is extraordinary concentration in a singled-out detail', juxtaposed with the photograph of a cyclist. In classic film realism the close-up image is incorporated metonymically into the main narrative, as in the films of Griffith. The close-ups in *Un chien andalou*, on the contrary, constitute breaks in the narrative. For example the sequence hole in hand – woman's armpit – sea-urchin presents a lateral development difficult to integrate into the main storyline. Apparently gratuitous, incongruous images distract from the unfolding of the drama the attention of the viewing subject, whose embodied gaze is literally fascinated or *seduced* by the image.[1] As a result the viewer loses track of the narrative. As a fragment that cannot be fully incorporated into a coherent narrative, and as a filmic element relatively free from the syntagmatic context, the close-up acquires a powerful material and semantic intensity. According to Aragon, the close-up magnifies and transforms objects that acquire as a consequence a new resonance, and 'take on menacing or enigmatic meanings' (Hammond 2000: 52). The isolation of the close-up from the diegetic unfolding of the plot thus opens it up to the possibility of metaphoric or symbolic associations. This is suggested by Dalí, who writes: 'A simple change of scale provokes unusual resemblances, and existing, though unimaginable, analogies' (Dalí 1998: 13) Hence, in the example cited above, the montage of ants – armpit – sea urchin, by intercalating the image of the woman's body-part between two images of animals, has the effect of alienating the woman from the human sphere, evoking her as animal, as other. The effect of the close-up, consequently, like that of repetition, is to displace the unfolding of the narrative, by focusing on the material, enigmatic or poetic qualities of the image. Finally, as will be argued later in this chapter, the close-up can be linked to a subjective point of view, suggesting the alternative space of the dream(like).

## A cinema of attractions

Buñuel recognized in Fritz Lang's *Der Müde Tod / Destiny* (1921) and *Metropolis* (1927) a 'disconcerting dualism' between the storytelling element and a 'pure lyrical', non-narrative dimension (Buñuel 2000: 99). A similar dualism is operative in *Un chien andalou*, where visual shocks, non-sequiturs and poetic associations do more than destabilize the conventional storytelling codes. They appear to have a logic of their own and point to an alternative distinctive temporality – immediate, elliptical, non-developmental – running parallel and counter to the temporal unfolding characteristic of narrative. In this context, it is significant that the film is largely known – particularly among a generation of viewers exposed to a culture of clips, overexposed to the film's most striking images before (or without) viewing the film in its entirety – as a succession of seemingly autonomous gags or shock shots, an anthology of surrealist clips: razor-and-eye, ants-in-hand, rotting-donkeys-on-pianos, books-into-guns, ants-into-armpit-into-sea-urchins. Marina Vaizey (1979) for instance comments on the screening of the film at the 1979 Dalí exhibition in Paris: 'The combination of deeply disturbing, repellent images flickering on the screen – a woman being grossly fondled; a severed eye; a dismembered hand; corpses – all observed by the spectators in exquisite comfort, is typically Dalí.' Several critics have considered the film as an anthology of isolated images, in a type of reading encouraged by Dalí and Buñuel themselves, whose account of the original idea for the film as two striking dream images abstracted from any narrative context was discussed in chapter 1. They may well have taken their lead from dada film-viewing practices, in particular from the example of Breton and Vaché zapping from one cinema to another in wartime Nantes, rejecting sustained narratives in favour of the succession of autonomous sequences and the incongruity of their personal magical film montage (Hammond 2000: 73). The creative misreadings cited in chapter 1 also belong to this type of response to the film. In his 1924 *Manifesto of Surrealism*, Breton privileges the impact of single images over the temporal unfolding of a story. He excoriates the nineteenth-century realist novel, proposing an aesthetics of instantaneity derived from dadaist strategies of shock, based on the notion of the image as the encounter between disparate realities, producing a *spark* (Breton 1972: 37). The montage of narrative fragments or short independent sequences – the gory crime, the androgyne's suicide, the murder – also recalls the short news reports of the popular press, many of which were reproduced in *La Révolution surréaliste*. In this context the film could be considered as a collage of such *chiens écrasés* or disconnected sensationalist news items.

The film's alternative temporality can be linked to the early 'cinema of attractions' (1896–1905), with its roots in fairground spectacle and vaudeville performances. Georges Méliès, a magician and director of the Théâtre Robert-Houdin in Paris turned film director and producer, made around 500 films between 1896 and 1912, of current events, everyday scenes, gags, magical transformations, juggling and dancing. Based on minimal narratives, these films privileged single tableaux, discrete events, an 'explosive, surprising, and even disorienting temporality', over the linear development of story-telling (Gunning 2004: 44). Film techniques were often transposed from nineteenth-century theatrical strategies, illusionistic devices such as multiple or conflicting perspectives or the doubling of the actor. Dissolves, used in early cinema, derived from magic lantern displays, where they were used for their trick effect to ensure the smooth transition between images (Ezra 2000: 30). The frontal shooting of the opening sequence in *Un chien andalou* recalls the staged frontality of Méliès' films, producing a deliberately theatricalizing effect. The direct confrontation with the spectator – both surgeon and patient face her! –

was rare in late 1920s' filming, which tended to ignore the presence of the spectator. Avant-garde film directors of the 1920s were attracted to turn-of-the-century cinema with its focus on short discrete sequences relatively free from the constraints of story-telling, and its self-reflexive strategies. Such processes were radicalized in Eisenstein's theory of the montage of attractions[2] and in dada and surrealist films such as René Clair's *Entr'acte* (1924) or Man Ray's *Emak Bakia* (1926), where they subvert the conventions of realism. In *Un chien andalou* the isolated gags (man dissecting eye, tie tying itself, man pulling impossible load, couple buried in sand), magical transformations (dismembered to whole woman, clothed to naked body, breasts to buttocks, books to guns, moth to monster) and exhibitionist strategies (frontal shots, static camera) recall early cinema's themes and theatrical processes (see chapter 3 for a discussion of intertextual allusions to the cinema of attractions).

Recent scholarship has questioned earlier theories of film spectatorship, whether the stereotype of diegetic absorption into the illusory space of the projected image as a replay of the shadow images of Plato's cave (Jean-Louis Baudry), or the voyeuristic-sadistic male gaze (Laura Mulvey). Miriam Hansen (1993), for example, links early cinema's fragmented and heterogeneous spectacle to postmodern spectatorship, a position which could be applied to *Un chien andalou*. In the film the direct confrontation with the spectator brutally or subtly disrupts diegetic absorption, undermining the conventional voyeuristic relation between the spectator and the classic film text, based on the unfolding of a coherent story. Further, disruptions on the diegetic level foreground the work of the signifier, preventing passive consumption of the film. Thus the film stages a tension between two distinct temporal structures, linear and non-linear, as well as two distinct modes of reading, absorption and display. The viewer is both drawn into the diegetic universe of the melodramatic plot, and jolted out of it through the film's disparate images. It can be read in terms of a dialectic interaction between narrative and attraction elements, two temporalities and their interferences, in which the continuous unfolding of a story intersects with the discontinuous images of spectacular, isolated scenes, hence the ambivalent position of the spectator confronted with a film that is both artisanal gag and unsettling mise en scene of violation to the body. This ambivalence of the viewer can be linked to Dalí's paranoia-criticism, in which the viewer is simultaneously actor and spectator, both involved in the events and critically detached from the narrative.

Such disruptions defamiliarize perception and destabilize the spectator, who is assaulted not only indirectly through the formal and narrative techniques enumerated above, but also quite directly, as in the violence of the eye-slitting scene (similar in effect to the cannon or boxing gloves aimed at the camera in Clair's *Entr'acte*), the confrontation with the female character as the active subject of the gaze. The spectator's initial passivity – encouraged by the intertitle 'Once upon a time' – is violently disrupted through the literal assault on her own eye. As Mary Ann Caws argues about the opening scene: 'What is blown up here, in the initial act, is the identification of the viewer and the screen image; what is produced by such an explosion is the very notion of the passive self' (1981: 141). Is it our eye which is slashed, our hand which does the slashing? Are we assaulted or complicitous in the assault on the eye of the other? The viewer identifies both with the sadistic action of the criminal (identifying with Buñuel's gaze in point-of-view shots) and the masochistic passivity of the victim (identifying with the mirror object of her gaze).

For Breton, 'what we valued most in [the cinema], to the point of taking no interest in anything else, was its *power to disorient*' (Hammond 2000: 73). Disorientation or *dépaysement* – with its point of departure in everyday reality and its point of arrival in the surreal – was considered a fundamental surrealist principle. Related to the concept of defamiliarization or *ostranienie* developed by Chklovski and the early Russian Formalists, it is based on the idea that the function of art is to counteract the automatization that deadens everyday perception, making us see anew rather than simply recognize. The formal strategies of defamiliarization outlined above – the film's ellipses and interpolated shots, its spatial incongruities, irrational associations, rhythmic structures, fragmentation – impede naturalization. As a consequence normal perception of narrative as an organizing principle – the (chrono)logical succession of events, the verisimilitude of actions and characters – is impossible, and the processes of cinematic narration are foregrounded. In

*Un chien andalou* the absence of diegetic coherence disorients the viewer. With its selfconscious editing techniques (rapid cuts, frequent dissolves, irrational juxtapositions or superimpositions), the film simulates early filming techniques, foregrounding the film-text as a product of bricolage, a collage of fragments which refuse to stick together. Thus the visibility of the cinematic apparatus exposes – or perversely celebrates? – the film's fetish function, preventing spectatorial identification with the screened fiction.

As a result, according to Vigo (1930), the eye-slitting scene 'leaves us with no alternative but to admit that we are committed, that we will have to view this film with something other than the everyday eye!' Normal viewing patterns are deliberately denied, and the mind seeks other modes of association, as Buñuel himself states:

> To produce in the spectator a state which chould permit the free association of ideas, it was necessary to produce a near traumatic shock at the very beginning of the film; hence we began it with a shot of an eye being very efficiently cut open. The spectator entered into the cathartic state necessary to accept the subsequent events of the film. (Aranda 1975: 67)

With its literal visual aggression, the opening sequence shakes the viewing subject out of her passive mode of perception. Such an assault on stable spectatorial positions disrupts the symbolic order, problematizing standard consumption of the film, and allowing the irrational to express itself. Deprived of a firm anchor in a familiar narrative, the viewer is disoriented and hence open to the poetic qualities of the film. As a consequence the mind seeks alternative forms of linking, for example in the free associations of the irrational and the dream. The film medium, perhaps more freely than other modes of aesthetic production, allows images to be juxtaposed according to an order different from conventional spatial and temporal structures, without the more constraining overt syntactic links characteristic, for example, of verbal discourse. Buñuel draws links between *Un chien andalou* and dreams when he refers to the origin of the scenario as the memory of two dream images. He further claims that the film follows the logic of the unconscious, in which the principle of free association reveals a new type of coherence: 'It doesn't make sense to refer to a lack of logical links in *Un chien andalou* [...] It's simply a surrealist film in which images, sequences, follow on from each other according to a *logical order*, whose expression depends on the unconscious, which has naturally got its own order' (Aub 1991: 52). Hence, where overt narrative coherence fails, a second, covert logic, the logic of the unconscious or of dreams, is freed to take over.

## Psychoanalytical readings

Such assertions might seem authoritative. How then does the viewer read these filmic images: as detective or dreamer? Is the film to be actively deciphered or passively absorbed? Buñuel's answer appears to be paradoxical. In 'Notes on the making of *Un chien andalou*' (1947), he claims that 'NOTHING, in the film, SYMBOLIZES ANYTHING', and that the images remain enigmatic to film-makers and viewers (Mellen 1978: 153). However, he also suggests in the same text that psychoanalysis might offer the only possible method of interpretation. Following Buñuel's lead, a number of critics have interpreted the film in the context of psychoanalysis. Two questions in particular have been explored when considering the work in this context: What does the film mean? How does the film function?[3] While a number of commentators have interpreted the film as the story of the psychosexual development of the main protagonist, others, focusing on the film's structure, have considered ways in which the film replicates dream mechanisms.

In the first place, the storyline has been described as a young man's experiences from infancy to maturity, as the tale of frustrated male desire, or as a young man's struggles with his homosexual desires.[4] In this context, the prologue invokes the primal scene, the sexual act or the castration complex. The male protagonist is seen initially as sexually undifferentiated (cyclist, androgyne), immature (child-adult, maternal role of woman), inhibited (masturbation suggested by hands, ants or cocktail shaker). The hero experiences a conflict between his homosexual and his heterosexual desires, as suggested by the figure of the androgyne. The young man tries to free himself from his inhibitions (seduction of young woman), but he is rejected. He is held back from approaching the woman by the power of the super-ego (donkeys-and-piano load), and regresses to an infantile stage (bed and frills) and onanism (ants again, mutilated hand). Once his tyrannical super-ego (the double) has been killed, he re-attempts seduction, but the young man fails to overcome his inhibitions and the woman rejects him (death-head moth sequence) and turns to another man. Alternately the young man experiences remorse (death-head moth sequence again) and finally overcomes his 'vice' (his trapped hand refers to his past actions, and his former self's clothes are thrown out the window or left to rot on the beach) thanks to the intervention of the female character. Only one critic has given the female character the central role, summarizing the story as a young woman's struggles with three men (Demeure 1954).

While some of these interpretations are grounded in a detailed discussion of the film, actions and objects are often read in terms of a simplistic one-to-one symbolism, whereby for example razor, hand, tie and cocktail shaker represent the penis, while eye and box represent the vagina; or gourds symbolize 'ancestral traditions', pianos 'immutable harmonies' and donkeys 'stupidity'.[5] The explanations offered by a mechanical application of psychoanalytical concepts tend to offer little more than an amateur diagnosis, reducing the film's complexity to a simple rebus, like the fixed symbolism of the 'key of dreams' popular in the 1920s. The film-maker Jean Epstein (1922) critiques early applications of Freudian psychoanalysis as a kind of detective work, 'the Nick Carter method'. Such readings all posit the principle of an unproblematic narrative coherence grounded on the psychology of the male protagonist's actions or on a unified point of view. Piazza (1949), for instance, claims that 'the disparate sequences do not manage to eliminate the underlying unity conferred by the main character's obsessional neurosis', while Edwards states that 'it is even possible – a measure of the film's innovative and thoroughly experimental character – to regard the whole of its action as the representation of the young man's confused and shifting thoughts from the moment of his first appearance on the bicycle' (1982: 52).

In his 1929 article 'An Andalusian Dog', Dalí writes scathingly about psychoanalysis: 'Psychoanalysis will be able to dismantle the subtlest of psychic mechanisms and to once again study human facts. But despite this, neither these facts nor the tongue of the anteater will become less enigmatic and irrational because of this' (1998: 109). It is well known that Buñuel would burst out laughing at interpretations that pinned down the film to a single psychoanalytical meaning. Indeed, he himself pastiches this type of reading in an interview:

> A cavalry captain from Saragossa, a German teacher and many other persons agreed on identical explanations: '*The man goes up to the woman equals sexual impulse. The ropes equal moral obstacles. The two corks: the frivolous life. The two dried pumpkins: testicles. The priests: religion. The piano: the lyricism of love. And the donkey: death.*' Instead of trying to explain the images, it would be better to accept them as such. We should be content to know if they repulse, move or attract us. (Aub 1991: 31)

The readings outlined above choose as a whole to bypass the continuously shifting points of view, particularly in the last part of the film where there is a shift from the woman as the object of male desire to the woman as the subject of her own fantasies and desires (see the analysis of the death-head moth sequence in chapter 3). More importantly, with its focus on the psychology of the individual, this type of reading domesticates the film, reducing it to little more than a psychological drama. This type of approach fails to take into account Buñuel and Dalí's deliberate pastiche of Freudian processes, their parodic reworkings of psychoanalytical syntax and symbols. Given their familiarity with Freudian ideas (Freud's *Interpretation of Dreams* had been translated into Spanish in 1925), *Un chien andalou* can justifiably be read as a fully conscious and playful accumulation of perversions of Freudian complexes (narcissism, infantilism, onanism, homosexuality, coitus interruptus, buried alive) and wordplay (*avoir des fourmis dans la main*, *coup d'oeil*[6]) packed into just seventeen minutes of film! For Robert Short, Buñuel and Dalí are 'gleefully laying on the Freudianisms with a parodic trowel' (2002: 74). The very proliferation of common sexual symbols – the severed hand, the holed hand, the slit eye – are scattered throughout the film like odd pieces of a jigsaw, the playful rewriting of the popular key of dreams. Indeed, allegorical interpretations are quite out of keeping with the film-makers' radical aim to shock and disturb, or indeed with the surrealist agenda of disruption which they purported to be responding to. Such interpretations do not take into account the search for a visual mode of expression as a direct assault on the viewer. Relevant to this debate is the dispute caused by Germaine Dulac's film production of Antonin Artaud's script *La Coquille et le clergyman / The Seashell and the Clergyman* (1928).[7] Artaud rejected Dulac's psychological interpretation of his script in favour of a cinematic expression which would evoke the 'birth of thought', the direct presentation of a fluid inner life, grounded on 'purely visual situations whose drama would come from a shock designed for the eyes, a shock drawn, so to speak, from the very substance of vision and not from psychological circumlocutions of a discursive nature which are merely the visual equivalent of a text' (Abel 1988: 411). Finally, such readings bypass the ludic dimension of the film, which can be read as a highly conscious parody of bourgeois realism and of the psychological intensity of Impressionist films (see chapter 3).

Rather than asking questions about the meaning of the film, a more fruitful approach by the viewer in her Nick Carter role might be to consider questions relating to the structure of the film. In 'Notes on the making of *Un chien andalou*', quoted earlier, Buñuel himself maintains that the plot 'does not attempt to recount a dream, although it profits by a mechanism analogous to that of dreams' (Mellen 1978: 151). His statement echoes Artaud's, for whom the screenplay of *The Seashell and the Clergyman* 'is not the re-creation of a dream and should not be considered as such. I shall not attempt to excuse its apparent incoherence by the facile subterfuge of dreams' (Abel 1988: 411).[8] This approach focuses less on the psychological processes or the *dream content* than on the structures of the processes of consciousness or the *dream work*. For Fieschi, for example, the film reproduces less the imagery of dreams than the mechanisms of the unconscious, its processes of condensation and displacement (1972: 82).

We should remember that film and psychoanalysis were contemporaneous developments, both elaborated in opposition to late nineteenth-century positivism. The Lumière brothers screened their first films in Paris in 1895; in the same year Breuer and Freud's *Studies on Hysteria* were published in Vienna. Contemporary discourse linked the film medium and dream mechanisms. In an article titled 'The Influence of Dream on the Cinema' (1925), Paul Ramain argued that film techniques are similar to dream processes: '*All the expressive and visual processes of the cinema are found in dream* [...] The simultaneity of actions, soft-focus images, dissolves, super-impositions, distortions, the doubling of images, slow motion, movement in silence – are these not *the soul of dream and daydream*?' (Abel 1988: 363). Parallels between the language of filmic processes and analytic language are evident in their shared visual metaphors ('projection', 'screen memories'), and links can be drawn between dream work and film mechanisms in such processes as condensation, displacement, and spatio-temporal distortion. Buñuel and Dalí's use of cinematic language thus belongs to the contemporary tendency to relate cinematography to dream mechanisms. Buñuel maintained that cinema is the best medium for expressing the world of dreams:

> Because of the way it works, the mechanism for producing film images is, of all the means of human expression, the one that is most like the mind of man or, better still, the one which best imitates the functioning of the mind while dreaming. [...] [A]s in the dream, the images appear and disappear by means of dissolves or fades-in and -out; time and space become flexible, contract and stretch at will, chronological order and relative values of duration no longer correspond to reality. (Hammond 2000: 114)

In this approach, the very elements that appear to impede the coherent development of narrative point instead to an alternative logic, that of the dream: the absence of cause-and-effect links can be read in terms of repression; spatio-temporal inconsistencies signal a shift from objective to subjective verisimilitude; the absence of closure of the narrative characterizes the discourse of desire, while radical montage suggests the mechanisms of desire.

The dreamlike in *Un chien andalou* is coded firstly through mise en scène, in the co-presence within the same frame of real and fantasy space, as in the sequence where the male protagonist drags a heterogeneous assemblage of objects within the confined space of the room; or in the scenes where ants swarm from a hole in his hand. More often, however, the dreamlike is suggested through editing processes, dream structures are emulated at the montage or *découpage* stage, 'the supreme instant of segmentation' (Buñuel 2000: 133). In an interview with Dalí, Buñuel states that he attaches 'absolute' importance to the photography and editing

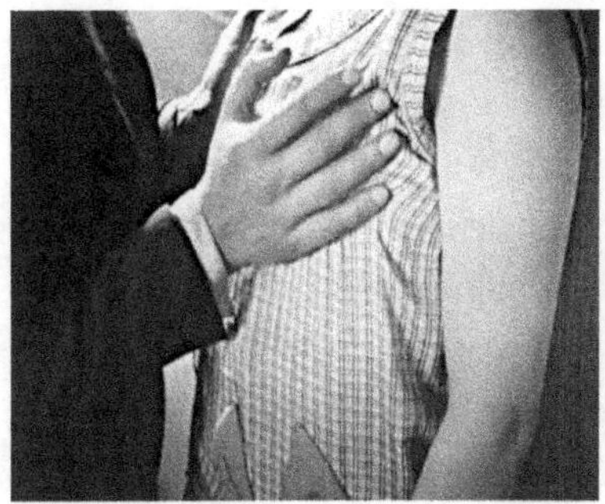

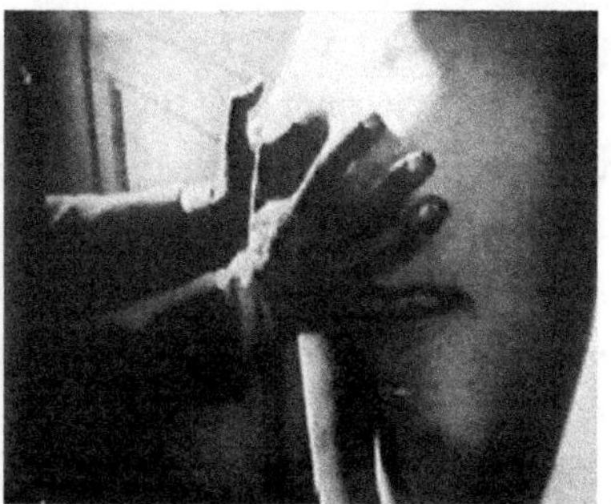

Breasts to buttocks

(Dalí 1998: 88). The dreamlike is thus suggested, precisely, through the montage techniques listed earlier in this chapter as elements of diegetic disruption – close-ups, dissolves, and non-diegetic cuts.

The emotive power of close-up shots such as the slashed eye, the severed hand, the hand with ants, armpit hair, depends both on the focus on the violated part-body, and on the compositional context – rhythmical or disruptive – within which the shots are inscribed. The close-up is often linked to alternating montage which gives it a strong emotive charge, as in the opening sequence, where the moon / cloud shots alternate with the eye / razor shots. The disturbing effect of the close-up of the death-head moth is created by the serial build-up of ever closer shots of the insect which acquires gigantic proportions, an effect underscored by the use of the iris shot and the overexposed shot.[9] Alternating montage reproduces the mechanisms of desire: for example, the shots of the couple at the window (off-screen look) alternate with the street scene and accident in a compulsive accelerated rhythm that appears to awaken the male protagonist's sexual desire. The soundtrack itself, a montage of Wagner's *Liebestod* and two Argentinian tangos, gives the film a sexual dynamics, alternating between the romantic, sublimated desire of the Wagner and the popular, carnal desire of the tangos. The real is also transformed into a space of fantasy through the technique of dissolve, as in the sequence where Batcheff caresses Mareuil's covered breasts which are transformed into naked breasts, then into buttocks; or the sequence where the hand with a hole swarming with ants dissolves into the woman's armpit hair, which in its turn dissolves into a sea-urchin, then into an iris shot of the androgyne with the severed hand. Thirdly, dissolves or cuts produce non-sequiturs: the temporal and spatial breaks discussed above in terms of disruption of the main narrative can be read in terms of the fragmented dream narrative. For example, when the male character dies, he falls first in the room, then in the park, his fall linking a real space with a fantasy space. Similarly, the female character leaves the apartment and steps into a seaside space in a single cut. Finally, the narrative – fragmentary, elliptical and incomplete – stages the themes of expectation and desire. The enigmatic structure constitutes a strategy that simulates and stimulates desire, and the constantly reactivated suspense and inconclusive endings intensify the sense of unfulfilled desire. The effect of montage is thus to mimic the processes of desire and dream, using a rhetoric of displacement and condensation.

The prologue has attracted extensive critical attention, indeed more has been written on the opening sequence than on any other aspect of the film. The screenplay presents the scene with clinical concision:

> ONCE UPON A TIME…
> A balcony. Night. A man is sharpening a razor by the balcony.
> The man looks through a window at the sky and sees…
> A light cloud passing across the face of the full moon.
> Then the head of a young woman with wide-open eyes. The blade of the razor moves towards one of her eyes.
> The light cloud now moves across the face of the moon. The razor-blade slices the eye of the young woman, dividing it.

The sequence's almost unbearable visual impact, its isolation from the rest of the film, and the many associations suggested by the sequence, present a challenge to viewer and critic. As a sexual image, it has been read as an allegory of childbirth (Mondragon), sexual intercourse (Durgnat, Renaud), as rape or castration (Williams), as a primal scene (Pérez), a scene of death (Iampolski), or an image of the destabilization of the male subject (Sandro). Other interpretations have focused on the literal and metaphorical assault on the eye of the spectator (Caws, Perrier, Thiher, Williams) and as a metaphor of inner vision (Vigo). The image of Buñuel's hand slicing the eye has been interpreted as an allegory of the filmic montage in which real images are cut up to produce new combinations

(Bonitzer, Farges, Williams), or a meta-discursive comment on film-making itself (Drouzy, Dubois).

Several critics have analysed the film as a whole in terms of the prologue, arguing that the narrative is generated by the initial sequence. Structuralist-psychoanalytical interpretations have been elaborated, informed by the work of Christian Metz, based on the premise of the generative function of the opening sequence. Fieschi, for instance, argues that the eye-slitting sequence puts in place two signifying chains, of desire and castration, engendering a series of images that structure the film. The eye as an 'instrument of desire' triggers the first chain of associations, which includes the ants in the hand, armpit hair, sea urchin, the 'hesitant choreography of desire'; while the movement of the razor across the eye sets off the 'chain of castration' – slit eye, fall from bicycle, chopped-off hand. The film's 'transgressive violence', Fieschi argues, lies in 'the faultless logic of its development'. Dramatic logic is anchored in, and displaced by, symbolic structures, through processes of displacement and condensation, exposing a subjective spatio-temporal reality governed by libidinal forces (Fieschi 1972: 82).[10]

The most elaborate and lucid analysis of the prologue is arguably that of Linda Williams (1981a), who interprets the film as a model psycho-analytical situation. She establishes in detail the methodological basis for her analysis of the 'dreamlike rhetoric' that structures the film, drawing on Freud's notion of the return of the repressed, Jakobson's work on metaphor and metonymy, paradigm and syntagm, and Lacan's analogy between rhetorical figures and primary processes in dreams. Freudian analysis develops the dual aspect of dream activity: in dreams the unconscious tries simultaneously to express itself and to cover this expression through the work of censorship. The prologue is thus read as a figure of castration, an initial loss which structures desire and generates the rest of the film. Since the initial traumatic scene of castration cannot be named directly, it is expressed indirectly in the rest of the film through processes of displacement and condensation. Williams contends that the narrative coherence of the film lies in its figural dimension, the repetition of the initial traumatic sequence by indirect means through figures of the fetish (frills and box as fetishistic substitutes for the cyclist, severed hands) and of sexual in/differentiation (cyclist wearing suit and tie and frills, androgyne, buttocks and breasts).

Paul Sandro's analysis (1987) draws on Williams' reading while extending the significance of the opening scene. He argues that the 'eye-I' of the prologue associates the gaze with the awareness of the self and the construction of identity. Sandro grounds his interpretation in Lacanian psychoanalysis, which posits three stages in the formation of individual identity: the first stage where the child is undifferentiated from the maternal entity; the mirror phase at around eighteen months, when the child's self-identity is constructed through processes of identification with, and differentiation from, the visual image of the (m)other; and the symbolic stage, marked by an awareness of lack and a desire to recover the whole body. For Sandro, the violation of the eye in the first sequence has unconscious associations with the threat of dismemberment (castration) and the disintegration of the self as a whole body, a seeing subject. Like Williams, Sandro reads the initial sequence as a trauma which is both repressed and indirectly expressed in the rest of the film. The traumatic scene returns firstly through the cuts and spatio-temporal disjunctions of montage, which disrupt narrative continuity, signalling that the diegesis has been colonized by the discourse of desire. Such 'lapses' in montage dismember the film body. Secondly, graphic repetition in the main body of the film recalls the prologue through processes of displacement, which repeat indirectly certain motifs of the prologue. Sandro gives the example of the diagonals of the opening sequence (striped tie, movement of man sharpening his razor) that reappear in displaced form (fall from bike, stripes on box, double falling). One could extend Sandro's analysis to include the recurrence of round shapes (sea urchin, armpit, the crowd around the androgyne and the severed hand, iris opening / closing shots). Thirdly the fragmented body parts of the prologue (eye and hand) resurface in images of dismemberment (the man's hand stuck in the door, the severed hand, hands cut off by framing), the migrant armpit hair, the image of the skull on the moth, the mouth effaced, the couple half-buried in sand, the wordgames (*dentelière* contains *dent* or tooth, *coup d'oeil* is taken literally as a blow to the eye). Moreover, the dissolution of the body is explicit in the images of the hand swarming with ants, the decomposing donkeys (the script added excrements!), the androgyne run over, the funeral procession or the couple's burial. The criminal of the opening sequence may well have disappeared from the screen, he continues to wield his scalpel, cinematically, slicing the eye, splicing the film.

The originality of readings grounded on the analysis of the opening sequence as a traumatic scene that generates and structures the rest of the film lies in their focus on the dream work (strategies of condensation or displacement) or psychoanalytical processes (repression, return of the repressed), showing how the film is structured as a simulacrum of psychic processes.[11] Their advantage over the allegorical readings discussed earlier is that they acknowledge the ambivalence of the images on the one hand, and account for the film's gaps and apparent inconsistencies on the other, thereby avoiding the shortcomings of a reductive reading. However, do the strategies of elucidation provided by psychoanalytical readings fully explain the strategies of confusion elaborated by Buñuel and Dalí? The readings outlined above tend to focus on recurrent motifs (repetition, variation, formal generation), paradigmatic structures which establish links across the whole filmic text, cutting across the narrative, constantly returning to the opening images (Sandro 1987: 48). For example, the association between eyes of woman – donkey – couple bypasses considerations of the syntagmatic organization or the immediate context within which these are inscribed. As a result the disjunctions, disparities, non-sequiturs or lateral developments appear to be ironed out, integrated into a totalizing reading. How does one integrate into such a reading the collective discourses, the intertextual references, the parodies of filmic conventions, the collaging of distinct filmic elements? Above all, to what extent do such readings take into account the self-conscious use of psychoanalytical discourse in the film (Thiher 1979: 35)? They may well be a response to the desire of the viewing subject for a coherent interpretation – Breton, for instance, declares that the mind is capable of establishing links between the most disparate realities – rather than to the material reality of the film with its non-sequiturs, arbitrary juxtapositions, shifts and slippages. In that case, these readings manifest a resistance to considering the filmic text in its irreducible heterogeneity and fragmentation, its plurality of associations and absence of closure.

## Symbols or material images?

The interpretations of the prologue outlined above, however convincingly argued, do not always take into account, with notable exceptions (Williams, Sandro) the fundamental ambivalence of the opening sequence, as an image of sadistic, destructive impulses (sexual penetration, male castration), and an image of the liberation of sight. The film invites interpretation, yet it resists a totalizing meaning. It resists interpretation, yet teases the spectator with a multiplicity of possible meanings. Graphic forms generate series of images or objects, disrupting the narrative, and resonating with other similar designs. The striped motif, for instance, migrates from the tie to the box to the wrapping paper and back to the tie, each contained within the other like a Chinese puzzle, the very repetition of the motif inviting interpretation – as if the viewer, like the female protagonist, could unpack a meaning from this Pandora's box – yet offering no clear meaning. The striped box tantalizes the viewer with the possibility of meaning while obstinately refusing to function as a fixed sign. It migrates from the cyclist to the apartment (where it is laid out on the bed), to the street again (where the severed hand is placed) and finally to the seashore. Props become fetishes become props again; they disintegrate and are finally abandoned. The process is actually thematized in the last sequence of the film, where earlier fetish objects – box, cord, tie, frills (the script added the bicycle, not shown in the film) – literally resurface, washed up by the sea as pieces of flotsam, picked up and thrown away, like empty props, reified signs of possible narratives, a return to the banality of the real, signs returning to objects, a variant now played out, but always open to reassembly. Similarly, the juxtaposition of woman's face and male hand in the opening sequence, potent with dramatic meaning, become the banal gestures of a lovers' meeting (with watch restored!) This suggests that Buñuel and Dalí are playing with signifying processes. Metonymic or simply syntagmatic links replace narrative logic, the proliferation – and consequent defusion or dissolution – of meanings impedes the linear unfolding of the story. The multiplicity of possible yet inconclusive referential or symbolic meanings itself frees the images from

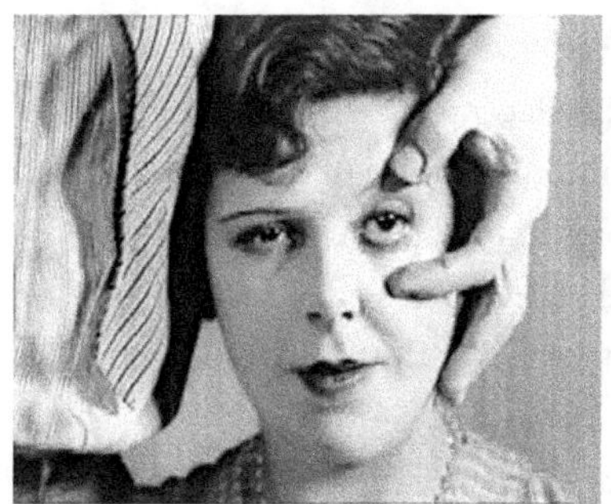
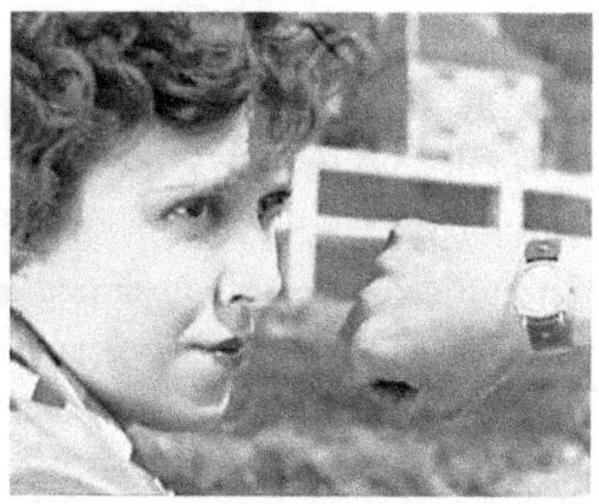

Eye and hand

any narrative function to float freely as itinerant signs, and the viewing subject is subjected to the delirious interpretations of Dalí's paranoia-criticism – or indeed confronted with the absence of meaning. Interpretations are all the more open since objects and actions are not firmly grounded in a fixed diegetic development. Untrammelled by syntactic constraints, they can proliferate freely. This characteristic of the film recalls the surrealists' with the single image, which is decontextualized and, as a consequence, remains open to multiple associations, like the covers of the popular Fantômas serialized publications such as *Le crime d'une brute* (1908) or *La main coupée* (1927), which so attracted the surrealists.

Two examples from the film will be used to exemplify the power of such open signifiers to engender multiple meanings: the shot of Vermeer's *Lacemaker* and the donkeys-and-pianos sequence, two images with strong cultural associations that are perverted by Buñuel and Dalí. The single shot in close-up of Vermeer's *Lacemaker* appears to run counter to the diegetic development, and its tenuous relation to the fictional context has given rise to a proliferation of interpretations, some apparently unrestrained by narrative constraints. One critic sees in the painting 'the figuration of the unconscious themes of perforation and chaining' (Piazza 1949: 149). The woman gazing at the reproduction of the painting mirrors the figure of the lacemaker absorbed in her work, both images suggesting narcissistic fulfilment; when the woman throws down the book, she substitutes narcissism for interpersonal desire (Sandro 1987: 46), or overthrows her inhibitions in favour of her instinctive feelings, in a transition from passive to sexually aggressive behaviour (Edwards 2004: 85). The painting refers to the myth of Penelope (Talens 1993: 50) or to death, a metaphoric substitute of the butterfly Athropos (Iampolski 1993). The lacemaker's costume is linked to that of the cyclist, interpreted as the subjective vision of the young woman (Drummond 2005: 110). An analogy is drawn between the power of the concentrated gaze of the painting and the young woman's fixed gaze on the fetish objects on the bed and an echo, in the woman absorbed by creative work, of Buñuel sharpening his razor (Leutrat 1993). It is, one must conclude, precisely in the absence of closure of the film's images and their multiple associations that the radical nature of the film resides. The viewer's desire inhabits the very gaps and fissures in the filmic text, amplifying its figural associations.

While the shot of Vermeer's painting interrupts the coherent unfolding of the storyline, the donkeys-and-piano sequence can be linked more easily to the diegetic. The screenplay presents the scene in even more dramatic detail than the film:

> The man begins advancing towards her, pulling at the rope and making a great effort to drag whatever is attached to the ropes. First we see a cork, then a melon, then two Catholic priests, then finally, two magnificent grand pianos containing the carcasses of two donkeys. Their feet, tails, rumps and excrement are spilling out of the lids. As one of the grand pianos is pulled past the camera, we can see the big head of one of the donkeys hanging down over the keyboard. The man pulls at this with great difficulty, straining desperately towards the young woman, knocking over chairs, tables, a standing lamp and other objects on his path. The rumps of the donkeys get caught in everything. A stripped bone hits the light hanging from the ceiling, so that it rocks from side to side until the end of the scene.

It has been most frequently interpreted as the weight of the hero's past holding him back from satisfying his desires, an interpretation summarized by Georges Sadoul (1949: 199): 'Love (the passion of the hero) and sexuality (the melons) are impeded (the ropes) by religious prejudice (the seminarists) and bourgeois education (the piano).' Indeed this sequence, perhaps more than any other in the film, has given rise to a number of creative misreadings. While the script indicates that the donkeys' 'feet, tails, rumps and excrement are spilling out of the [piano] lids', and Dalí envisaged four pianos, the film leaves out the excrement and produces only two pianos. But viewers themselves have felt less constrained, and provided the excesses themselves, replacing donkeys by a deer, a horse or a

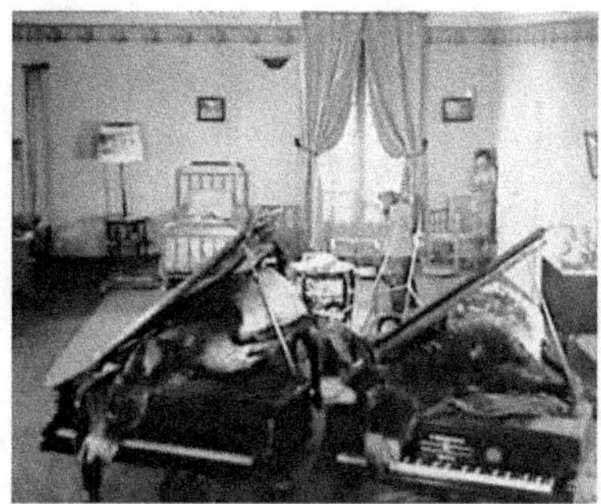
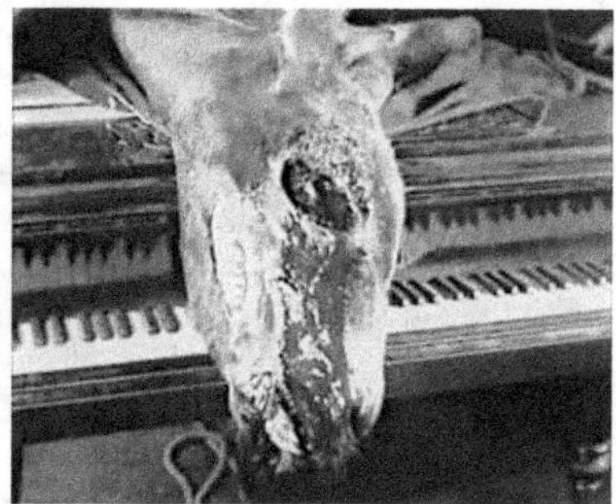

Pianos and donkeys

calf, adding giraffes and crocodiles, making the priests drag along the burden (see Drummond 1977: 73–5). However, in spite of the multiplicity of misreadings and possible meanings suggested by this sequence, no single reading can conjure away the materiality of the signifier – the concrete presence of the putrefying donkeys, the humorous assemblage of melons, corks and startled priests, 'at once archetypal surrealist installation and bachelor machine' (Short 2002: 95), the exaggerated Herculean straining of the male protagonist. In this scene, as in the opening sequence, there is both an urge to interpret on the part of the viewing subject, and a strong resistance to interpretation in the images themselves, a tension between symbolic meaning and material presence.

A number of silent film critics focused on film as a material reality, as opposed to film as a signifying reality. In an article titled 'Surrealism and Cinema' (1925), for example, Jean Goudal argued that film resists interpretation: 'In the cinema, as in the dream, the *fact* is complete master. Abstraction has no rights. No explanation is needed to justify the heroes' actions' (Hammond 2000: 88). This notion is echoed in Dalí's texts of 1927–28, where he proclaims that the freedom of the imagination is a consequence less of the subjectivity of the surrealist unconscious than of the objectivity of the 'poetry of facts'. He contrasts painting with photography and film, noting that the potentials of the latter 'are to be found in that unlimited imagination which is born of things themselves' Dalí 1998: 27). His description of the shooting of the film emphasizes the gory details:

> The shooting of the scene of the rotten donkeys and the pianos was a rather fine sight, I must say. I 'made up' the putrefaction of the donkeys with great pots of sticky glue which I poured over them. Also I emptied their eye-sockets and made them larger by hacking them out with scissors. In the same way I furiously cut their mouths open to make the white rows of their teeth show to better advantage, and I added several jaws to each mouth so that they were still vomiting up a little more of their own death, above those other rows of teeth formed by the keys of the black pianos. The whole effect was as lugubrious as fifty coffins piled into a single room. (Dalí 1968: 213)

Similarly, for Artaud, writing about his script *The Seashell and the Clergyman*, film is essentially a material reality, producing situations created by the 'mere collision' of incongruous elements: 'And because it works with matter itself, cinema creates situations that arise from the mere collision of objects, forms, attractions, repulsions. It does detach itself from life, but rediscovers the original order of things.' (Abel 1988: 412). Until recently, however, little critical attention has been paid to the direct impact of the film's images, the 'jolt of pure presence' of the montage of attractions (Gunning 2004: 48), the material presence of bodies rotting, swarming, migrating, dissolving, which defy interpretation. In his reassessment of the film Ian Walker shifts from the focus on meaning to the direct impact of a physical action, for 'no "symbolic" reading may halt the movement of that razor' (Walker 1977: 5). Similarly, Williams argues that, in spite of the allusions to fears of castration or of penetration (which she had analysed in her earlier studies on the film), 'the codes and sexual contexts offer no clear image of this either. These are images made flesh, elements of a violent visual theory played out like a mystery play' (Williams 1994: 16). More recently, Jonathan Jones (2004) – in an aptly named article, 'The Joy of gore' – stressed the physicality of the images: 'What we see is a drama of physical things: the moon and a cloud, a razor and an eye. It's not symbolic, but instantly visceral.' For Jones, the physical world is less a ground for the setting of the characters' actions, than a resistant space, 'an opaque field of desire in itself', and he contrasts the 'cloacal, bloody texture' of the film with Hollywood's more aseptic 'unreality'. It is this quality of the film's images – their literal, material presence – which is eclipsed in the psychoanalytical readings outlined above, but which is suggested for example in the repeated allusions to the 'poetic' qualities of the film. While symbols demand an interpretation, poetic images remain enigmatic and retain their materiality.

The materiality or viscerality of the film can in fact be linked to the dissident surrealist Georges Bataille's concepts of 'base materialism', or what resists symbolization or sublimation, and the 'formless', that which resists processes of ordering or naming, concepts developed in a series of essays published in the journal *Documents* in 1929–30. His own commentary on *Un chien andalou* appeared in an article entitled 'Oeil'/ 'Eye', and it echoes Dalí's text quoted above: 'Several very explicit facts appear in successive order, without logical connection it is true, but penetrating so far into horror that the spectators are caught up as directly as they are in adventure films. Caught up and even precisely caught by the throat, and without artifice' (Bataille 1985: 19). For Bataille the transgressive violence perpetrated on the eye is linked both to horror and seductiveness, for 'extreme seductiveness is probably at the boundary of horror'. On the page facing Bataille's article is a reproduction of Dalí's painting *Blood is Sweeter than Honey* (1927), whose motifs – eye-socket, dagger, hand – anticipate the images of *Un chien andalou*. In 'Lugubrious Game', Bataille's discussion of Dalí's paintings – which underlines images of putrefaction, bestiality, dismemberment and abjection – alludes to the violence of Dalí's gesture: 'Dalí's razors carve into our faces the grimaces of horror that probably risk making us vomit like drunkards this servile nobility, this idiotic idealism that leaves us under the spell of a few comical prison bosses' (Bataille 1985: 28). Bataille's reading of Dalí's paintings is mediated through *Un chien andalou*'s violent imagery, as well as de Sade's images of mutilation and violence. The mutilation of the eye is a recurrent theme in Bataille's texts, notably in *L'Histoire de l'oeil / The Story of the Eye* (1928), where he challenges the primacy of vision, the Cartesian tradition of ocularcentrism, and returns to the corporeal, the body as grotesque form, lacking fixed boundaries. Bataille's texts, written partly in response to Breton's 'idiotic idealism', reject the metaphorical – and hence the sublimation of the image – favoured by Breton and the 'orthodox' surrealists. For Bataille, metaphor represses materiality. In an article titled 'Putrefying donkey', published in the first issue of *Le Surréalisme au service de la révolution* (1930), Dalí declares that the rotting donkey is a real image, 'truly and horribly rotting and covered with thousands of flies and ants', echoing Bataille's notion of 'base materialism'. Yet he also appears to defend Breton's notion of the sublimated image in his claim that the rotting donkey is a symbolic image: 'And we do not know whether behind the three great simulacra – shit, blood and putrefaction – there does not lie the very hiding place of the sought-after "treasure land".' (1998: 117) In a Bataillean reading of the film, Martin Jay focuses on the visceral, sadistic dimension of the film, and in particular on the initial act's literal dimension, referring to 'the third eye of the seer [...] deprived of its spiritualizing, elevating function', and concluding that the 'Icarian flights of Breton's seer end in the bowels of Bataille's labyrinth' (Jay 1994: 259–60).

The materiality of the images is enhanced by their isolation from the logic of the narrative. For example the very lack of a rational justification for the presence of putrefying donkeys in an apartment underscores their simple being-there, while the iris shots of the close-up of the death-head moth isolates it from diegetic continuity, focusing on its monstrous presence. Above all, the eye-slitting scene itself is structured as a series of breaks in the diegesis. At first, following the opening intertitle 'Once upon a time', the spectator is lulled into the expectation of a timeless story, further encouraged by the romantic image of the moonlit night, which draws the viewing subject passively, unwittingly, into the narrative space. She is then jolted out of the illusory space by the break in the diegesis represented by the eye-slitting scene, narratively disconnected both from what precedes – albeit formally, almost risibly, generated by the moon-cloud image – and from what succeeds it (the temporal break marked by 'Eight years later'). The spectator is assaulted by the brutal presence of an image without a frame or context. The action, devoid of a justification, is thus present in all its violence and materiality.

Finally, the complexity of the critical apparatus constructed around *Un chien andalou* may well make us forget that the production of the script and film was a good-humoured affair. The subversive potential of laughter, linked to the suspension of reason and the freeing of the irrational, should therefore not be underestimated. Resisting hermeneutical processes, laughter celebrates presence and materiality, valorizes contradiction and heterogeneity, liberates the grotesque, the ironic, the pastiche and the pun. And although laughter itself risks being retrieved by interpretive systems, the film constantly reactivates the ludic, the raw violence and vitality of images, in spite of the critical discourses which have sought to contain it. The playfulness of parody and pastiche – powerful forces of cultural subversion – will be the subject of the next chapter.

## Notes

1 See Bataille (1985: 22).
2 See Eisenstein (1988).
3 See Powrie (1998).
4 For this type of reading see: Mondragon (1949), Piazza (1949), Renaud (1963), Cesarman (1976), Drouzy (1978), Edwards (1982).
5 For example: 'the possession of the hand (the male sexual organ) in the box (vagina) signifies her [the androgyn's] physical possession of her lover' (Edwards 1982: 49).
6 For an analysis of the verbal expressions or 'babble' beneath the visual images of the film, see Liebman (1996).
7 For an analysis of the Dulac–Artaud dispute see Flitterman-Lewis (1996).
8 Unlike the rest of the surrealist group, who had rejected Dulac's film, Buñuel (1984: 106) had liked it. The box with the severed hand recalls the image of the head in the glass jar. Moreover, Bunuel's statement, quoted earlier, that his film is structured according to the logic of the unconscious, resonates with the press release for *The Seashell and the Clegyman* (quoted by Flitterman 1996: 111).
9 See Dalí, 'Photography, pure creation of the mind' (Dalí 1998: 12–14).
10 See also Marie (1981), Murcia (1994: 51), Edwards (2004: 82–3).
11 Other psychoanalytical analyses of the film include those by Drouzy (1978), Oswald (1981), Talens (1993).

# 3 Contexts and intertexts: between Fantômas and the fairground

> We have no talent – we who in our works have made ourselves the voiceless receptacles of so many echoes.
> André Breton

The first chapter recounted how the script of *Un chien andalou* was conceived and realized in terms of a montage of dreamlike images, deliberate disruptions, and irrational associations. This myth of origins was peddled by Buñuel and Dalí in their claim that the writing of the script was based on the surrealist model of automatism. Buñuel further claims all images and ideas with cultural associations were rejected: 'We wrote accepting the first images that occurred to us, systematically rejecting everything deriving from culture or education' (Turrent and Colina 1993: 30). This suggests that the script was produced in a vacuum, unmediated through social and cultural filters, echoing Surrealism's own myth of the blank sheet of paper or canvas as a starting-point for the work. Yet the script and film actually constitute a dense network of cultural allusions – quotations from other films, references to the film-makers' earlier texts and iconography, and allusions to the cultural context of the Spanish avant-garde and the surrealist movement. Indeed, by the end of the 1920s, the surrealists had acknowledged that 'pure' automatism was impossible, and that the texts they produced were in fact inscribed within a network of cultural allusions, infiltrated with quotations, pastiches, and traces of earlier texts. In other words, the automatic text itself is situated within an intertextual space. Intertextuality considered as the point of intersection of collective and often jarring voices questions and displaces the claims made by Buñuel and Dalí that the script and film were products of individual subjectivities, and calls into question critical assumptions regarding the ultimate homogeneity of the film.

This chapter aims to complement and critique the largely anecdotal history of the film's production outlined in chapter 1 by considering it as a product of the cultural context of the 1920s. As John Baxter, for instance, writes: 'many of the film's images came from the same pool of movie stills, advertising layouts, art prints and visual bric-à-brac which René Magritte, Max Ernst, Man Ray and a dozen other Surrealists had been plundering for years' (Baxter 1994: 77). The film will, therefore, be discussed in relation to Buñuel and Dalí's earlier texts and iconography and to the collective images of both the student group from the Residencia de Estudiantes and the surrealist group. They adopted conscious strategies in their film, parodying contemporary film genres: American comedy, avant-garde abstract cinema, expressionist and melodramatic film. They also turned to pre-war popular entertainment, the fairground images of their childhood, the films of Georges Méliès and Louis Feuillade. Finally the film will be assessed within the broader social and ideological context of the 1920s. Far from denying cultural and filmic history, it will be argued, *Un chien andalou* is woven into the cultural fabric, reflecting, revising and revitalizing it, often in a parodic mode. It will become clear that Buñuel and Dalí exploit both automatic and intertextual processes to subversive ends: automatism calls into question conventional discursive strategies dominated by logic and coherent expression, while intertextuality can be considered as a form of critical rereading or perversion of earlier texts and films. Both unsettle fixed positions and open up the frontiers of the possible.

## Spanish contexts

The film contains a network of allusions to Dalí and Buñuel's childhood and student days and to their iconographic and poetic production, as well as to the milieu of the Residencia de Estudiantes in Madrid, the 1920s' Madrid and Catalan avant-garde context, and the wider Spanish cultural field. These contexts intersect and dialogue within script and film.[1]

Buñuel's childhood and adolescence were permeated with images of death, sexuality and religion. 'Death [...] along with profound religious faith and the awakening of sexuality constituted the dominating force of my adolescence', he wrote (Buñuel 1984: 11). He attended a Jesuit college in Saragossa from 1906 to 1908 and his strict Catholic education may in part explain the violent anti-clericalism expressed in his films and texts. In his films death and sexuality are often related, as he himself recognized: 'I also have always felt a secret but constant link between the sexual act and death. I've tried to translate this inexplicable feeling into images, as in *Un chien andalou* when the man caresses the woman's bare breasts as his face slowly changes into a death mask. Surely the powerful sexual repression of my youth reinforces this connection.' (Buñuel 1984: 15) The film contains several satirical allusions to Catholic iconography. The severed hand, for instance, recalls medieval paintings of Christ's Passion; the male protagonist's outstretched arms holding books / guns allude to the Crucifixion of Christ; the hand crawling with ants suggests the stigmata, desublimated in an image of decomposing flesh; the striped box with its fetish contents is handled like a mock reliquary. The scene in which the male protagonist drags forward the heavy load of pianos-and-donkeys can be read as a parody of a religious procession, recalling Buñuel's childhood memory of a cartoon in the anarchist journal *El Motín* representing 'two well-fed priests sitting in a small cart while Christ, harnessed to the shafts, sweats and grimaces with the effort' (Buñuel 1984: 16).

A number of images in *Un chien andalou* can also be related to Buñuel's poems. A recurrent image for example is that of Marist priests, as in the following text, where Catholicism is satirized in a story of the absurd antics of two priests:

> Two Marists, prepared to risk their lives, were riding in a streetcar. They got off at the first stop and took another streetcar, full of beehives. The bees made a wonderful noise and the Marists laid themselves to rest in their coffins, prepared to risk everything. (Buñuel 2000: 30)[2]

The priests' situation anticipates their appearance in a similarly ludicrous posture in *Un chien andalou.* Above all, the image of the violated eyes recurs in Buñuel's texts. For example, 'Palacio de hielo' / 'Palace of Ice' (1927), from the collection of (unpublished) poems *Un perro andaluz*, narrates a violent event which can be considered as an early, equally gruesome, version of the opening sequence of the film:

> [...] Near the door a hanged man dangles over the enclosed abyss of eternity, howling for a long while. It's me. It is my skeleton with nothing left now but the eyes [...] The window opens and a lady appears filing her nails. When she considers them sharp enough she tears out my eyes and throws them into the street.
>
> My empty sockets remain, no gaze, no desires, no sea, no little chicks, no nothing. (Buñuel 2000: 60)

Far from being exclusive to Buñuel, such images were shared with Dalí, indicating a rich imaginative complicity between the two men. The theme of the violation to the eye appears in Dalí's own texts prior to 1929, as in the prose poem 'My girlfriend and the beach' (1927), with its image of a cataract operation; the text also includes a rotting donkey, swarming ants compared to the 'silent rhythm of sea urchins', and holes in the body (Dalí 1998: 21). Another prose poem, 'Christmas in Brussels' (1927), opens with the striking image: 'A hair in the middle of the eye. I give Anna my handkerchief so that she can remove it with the corner. An eye open wide with a hair across it' (Dalí 1998: 21).

Several images in the film can be linked to recurrent themes in Dalí's early paintings, in particular images of severed or decaying body-parts. The artist later claimed that *Un chien andalou* was an animated Dalí painting! (Dalí 1976: 76) The image of the erased mouth is present in the early *Selfportrait with 'L'Humanité'* (1923), while in *Portrait of Luis Buñuel* (1924) a long narrow cloud is represented level with Buñuel's right eye; the severed hand appears in *Apparatus and Hand* (1927); *Cenicitas* (1927) contains images of ants and severed limbs; while the rotting donkey is found in *Honey is Sweeter than Blood* – which also includes ants and severed hands – and *The Putrefied Donkey* (1928). Similar images also appeared in paintings and poems from 1929, produced at the same time as the script and film: ants and part-bodies in *The Great Masturbator*, cyclists in *Illuminated Pleasures,* a severed hand in *The Lugubrious Game*. A poem from 1929 contains the striking image: 'Why, after going around picking up cork crumbs from the ground, did I end up with a hole in the middle of my hand, filled with a compact and teeming anthill that I try to scoop out with a spoon?' (Dalí 1998: 81). Not only can a number of images thus be traced to the texts and paintings of the two film directors, but the absence of narrative coherence and the parodic tone of the film echo the disruption of logic and pastiche in the earlier works.[3] *Un chien andalou* in its turn was a source for further developments in Dalí's paintings and Buñuel's films in the 1930s and later (see Conclusion). It can, therefore, be considered as a crossroads where the images and obsessions of Dalí and Buñuel meet, mingle and, finally, diverge.

The themes which have been traced in the work of Buñuel and Dalí can also be related to their student days at the Residencia in Madrid. In the students' annual production of *Don Juan Tenorio* of 1921, Buñuel acted the part of Don Juan, who raped and murdered countless women, before being saved after death by a woman's love – a fitting rehearsal for his cameo role in *Un chien andalou*![4] The scene of the cyclist on the bed recalls one of the Resi's morbid rituals, where Lorca would lie on a bed as if dead; his friends would place him in an improvized coffin which they carried down into the street (Baxter 1994: 25). Fellow-student José Moreno Villa recounts a dream where he accidentally cut his eye with his razor while shaving. Beyond the anecdotal level, however, obsessive images of rotting carcasses, gouged-out eyes, and morbid sexuality were frequent in the poems, letters and dreams of the group of students. The image of the rotting donkeys is a model example of the intersection between individual and collective memories or fantasies. In his autobiography, for instance, Buñuel relates an incident from his childhood which was a source of horror and fascination:

> A dead donkey lay about a hundred yards away, swollen and mangled, serving as a banquet for a dozen vultures, not to mention several dogs. The sight of it both attracted and repelled me […] I stood there hypnotized, sensing that

> beyond this rotten carcass lay some obscure metaphysical significance. (Buñuel 1984: 11)

Dalí, for his part, records a coincidence regarding images of decay. In 1927, while he was painting images of rotting donkeys covered with flies, he received letters from Buñuel and Pepin Bello (whose poetic images of *putrefactos* profoundly impressed Dalí), both referring to similar images (Dalí 1998: 83). Moreover, fellow-students Dalí, Buñuel, Lorca and Viçens, out walking in the mountains near Madrid, would sometimes come across trenches where the peasants abandoned their dead animals, an encounter which gave rise to macabre jokes among the group (Morris 1972: 120–1). Dalí himself used the image of rotting donkeys in 'New limits of painting' (1928), where it is cited as an example of the rejection of rational associations in favour of the irrational and the arbitrary: 'we would add that a figure without a head is more apt to intersect with rotting donkeys and that flowers are intensely poetic, precisely because they resemble rotting donkeys' (Dalí 1998: 29). Dalí's position here can be linked both to an ongoing dialogue with Bataille's notion of the *informe*, and with a parallel development of the notion of putrefaction, which was linked to 'the entire world of rotting things: the transcendental and whimpering artists, far removed from all clarity, cultivators of all germs [...] the families who buy *objets d'art* to put on the piano' (Dalí 1998: 8). During their student days in Madrid, Buñuel, Lorca and Dalí had, in fact, developed the character of the *putrefact* linked to the notion of sentimental poetry and bourgeois decadence, exploiting it as a contrast with the notion of clarity and objectivity.

Beyond the little circle of Madrid students, the images which have been discussed can also be approached via a broader Spanish cultural tradition: the work of Cervantes (the picaresque mode), Goya (his paintings of animal carcasses, his grotesque images), or Velazquez (the tactile quality and obsessive observation of detail of his paintings); and via Ramón Gómez de la Serna's images of violence (razors, mutilated eyes) and his concept of *greguería* (the juxtaposition of disparate objects).[5] The poet Rafael Alberti (perhaps rather chauvinistically) defends a specifically Spanish version of Surrealism, closer to Goya than to French Surrealism, and claims that *Un chien andalou* expressed the state of mind of young artists and poets of the time (Morris 1972: 45). Similarly, for Aranda, the spatio-temporal disruptions can be linked to a specifically Spanish theatrical and narrative tradition, while he links the roots of the tactile quality of the images to traditional Spanish art (1975: 66–7). Dalí can be seen to corroborate this approach, citing at length a review of the film by Eugenio Montes, poet and fellow-student, who linked the film to the harshness of Spanish culture (quoted in chapter 1). And Dalí himself, in characteristically ebullient mode, relates the film to the violent history of Spain:

> *Le chien andalou* was the film of adolescence and death which I was going to plunge right into the heart of witty, elegant and intellectualized Paris with all the reality and all the weight of the Iberian dagger, whose holt is made of the blood-red and petrified soil of our pre-history, and whose blade is made of the inquisitorial flames of the Holy Catholic Inquisition mingled with the canticles of turgescent and red-hot steel of the resurrection of the flesh. (Dalí 1968: 212)[6]

## Surrealist iconography

It was suggested in chapter 2 that the theme of the eye in the film can be linked to a complex network of associations. The opening sequence has been read both as a violation to the eye and as the ritualistic opening of the eye onto new ways of seeing. A similar ambivalence is attached to the image of the eye throughout surrealist iconography and thought.[7] On the one hand the motif of the violated eye is recurrent in Surrealism: in Georges Ribemont-Dessaignes' play *L'Empereur de Chine* (published in 1921) a glass eye is enucleated, heads are chopped off, and a couple is buried in the sand; Max Ernst's illustration for the cover of *Répétitions* (1922) represents an eye with a piece of string threaded through it (the disembodied hand manipulating the string recalls the hand in the opening sequence of the film); in Man Ray's *Object to be destroyed* (1923) a woman's eye is cut out of a photograph and attached to the pendulum of a metronome; Breton notes how Nadja as a little girl gouged out her doll's eyes to see what was behind them. Buñuel kept Benjamin Péret's poems constantly in mind when making *Un chien andalou* and 'Les odeurs de l'amour' / 'The smells of love' most probably found an echo in the script: 'What greater pleasure / than to make love / the body wrapped in string / the eyes closed by razors' (Péret 1927: 167). The film's lateral associations can be seen as a transposition of the syntactical structures and associative patterns of Péret, a poet considered by Buñuel as the 'quintessential surrealist poet'. While they were writing the script in early 1929, Dalí and Buñuel would read poems from Péret's *Le Grand Jeu* which would make them 'weep with laughter' (Buñuel 1984: 110), and they enjoyed the poet's perverse 'convulsive' humour. And one final example: Bataille's novella *Histoire de l'oeil* (published in 1928) describes a violent scene which has clear affinities with the opening sequence of the film:

> On my asking what the word *urinate* reminded her of, she replied *terminate*, the eyes, with a razor, something red, the sun. And *egg*? A calf's eye, because of the colour of the head (the calf's head) and also because the white of the egg was the white of the eye, and the yolk the eyeball. The eye, she said, was egg-shaped [...] She played gaily with the words, speaking of *broken eggs*, and then *broken eyes*.

Behind many of these images, finally, lies the scene from Eisenstein's *Battleship Potemkin* (1925), in which the Cossack soldier blinds the old woman, a film the surrealists had retrieved from among the 'unbelievable cretinization' of 1920s' film production. Thus, the surrealist motif of the eye is seen to be intertwined with numerous other images, revealing an intricate network of intertextual links between verbal and visual texts.

The recurrent motif of the eye in Surrealism can also be read as a metonymy for a new vision, and the idea of the cinema as the 'new eye of man' (Soupault) was thematized in the opening shots of several dada and surrealist films of the 1920s. These often present the film director's camera as an extension of his eye: for example, the opening shot of *Emak Bakia* shows a cameraman in profile (the director Man Ray himself) operating a film camera, reflected in a mirror, yet the lens is pointed forward, towards the spectator, and an inverted eye is superimposed on the lens. This image is balanced by the final shot of the film showing the dancer Kiki de Montparnasse with eyes at once closed and open (the image of open eyes is painted onto her eyelids), thus dissolving fixed categories in a surrealist resolution of opposites. Similarly, in *Ballet mécanique* (1924), Fernand Léger films his own reflection in a deforming mirror. Such images draw attention both to the mechanics of filming and to image-making as creation and fabrication.

### A parody of 1920s' films

Although Buñuel would later claim that when he wrote the script for *Un chien andalou* he knew very little about film, the many references to film counter the claim and testify to the fact that, by 1929, he already had considerable knowledge of cinema. He had in fact acquired an extensive experience of films, and indeed the theatre, as a production assistant, critic, programmer and scriptwriter.[8] When he went to Paris in 1925 he enrolled as a student at Jean Epstein's Film Academy. He worked as an assistant and an extra on Epstein's *Mauprat* (1926), and briefly as second assistant on *La Chute de la maison Usher* / *The Fall of the House of Usher* (1928), before falling out with the director. He was an extra in Jacques Feyder's *Carmen – Espagne oblige* (1926) and an assistant on Henri Etiévant and Mario Nalpas' *La Sirène des tropiques* (1927) with well-known actors Pierre Batcheff, Simone Mareuil and Josephine Baker, and cameraman Albert Duverger. From 1927 he wrote film reviews for *La Gaceta Literaria Hispanoamericana* and articles on film aesthetics for *Les Cahiers d'art*, which discussed the influence of contemporary writers on film such as Epstein and Eisenstein. Thanks to his press card Buñuel would see up to three films a day, including private screenings of American films. As to the films seen, he was particularly struck by Sergei Eisenstein's *Battleship Potemkin*, F.W. Murnau's *Der Letzte Mann* / *The Last Laugh* (1924) and films by German film directors Georg Wilhelm Pabst and Fritz Lang. It was after viewing Lang's *Destiny* (1921) that Buñuel decided to become a director himself. His film reviews of the time include Erich von Stroheim's *Greed* (1924), Abel Gance's *Napoléon* (1926), Buster Keaton's *College* (1927), Victor Fleming's *The Way of All Flesh* (1927), and Carl Dreyer's *La Passion de Jeanne d'Arc* (1928). Buñuel admired the American school of cinema – Keaton, Menjou, Langdon – for their qualities of 'vitality, photogenia, a lack of noxious culture and tradition', contrasting them with the sentimentalism, literature and tradition of European cinema

(Hammond 2000: 61–2). He expressed his admiration for Griffith's filming techniques and rejected 'ostentatious' techniques. He was fascinated by the poetic potential of film, finding in Harry Langdon's films 'the new poetry [...] the equivalent of surrealism in cinema' (Buñuel 2000: 124). It was little wonder, then, that *Un chien andalou* should feature on a double bill with a Harold Lloyd comedy at its first run at Studio 28. Further evidence of his involvement is provided by the fact that with Ernesto Gimenéz Caballero he set up the first Spanish cine-club in 1927 at the Residencia de Estudiantes in Madrid where he had been a student. In 1929 he lectured on the avant-garde cinema at the Residencia, and screened René Clair's *Entr'acte* (1924), an extract from Jean Renoir's *La Fille de l'eau* (1924) and Alberto Cavalcanti's *Rien que les heures / As Time goes by* (1926). *Un chien andalou* itself followed two aborted film projects: a screenplay for a film on *Goya,* abandoned for lack of funding; and a screenplay *Caprichos*, based on Ramón Gómez de la Serna's short stories, for which he received 25,000 pesetas from his mother (which he was to use to fund *Un chien andalou).*

Buñuel was, moreover, involved in theatre production.[9] In 1926 he produced the set design for a stage production in Amsterdam of Manuel de Falla's opera *El Retablo de Maese Pedro / Master Pedro's Puppet Show*, based on an episode from Cervantes' *Don Quichotte.* Interpreted in part by puppets, it may well have influenced the exaggerated gestures of the characters in *Un chien andalou* and *L'Age d'or.* The following year he adapted *Hamlet,* performed in the basement of the Café Select in Montparnasse; its collage structure, dreamlike atmosphere and absurd situations can be seen to anticipate *Un chien andalou.*

Dalí, too, was a cinephile before turning to film-making himself. He wrote several articles on photography and film. In 'Photography: pure creation of the mind' (September 1927), for instance, he praises the '[p]ure objectivity of the little camera' and condemns 'the murky processes of the subconscious' (Dalí 1998: 12–13). In 'Film-arte, film-antiartistico'/ 'Art films, anti-artistic spool' (December 1927), on the other hand, he focuses on the ability of the cinema to transform everyday objects: 'The tree, the street, the rugby match are transubstantiated in a disturbing way in film' (Dalí 1998: 23). In the same article, he writes disparagingly about the 'artistic' film director who 'shoots at fake Cubist birds and hunts after a useless brick', preferring the 'anti-artistic' director who 'shoots at a brick wall and hunts unexpected and authentic Cubist birds'.[10] Like Buñuel, he expressed his preference for the more 'authentic' American comedy over European cinema, and the naturalism of popular films over the aestheticism of the avant-garde cinema. For Dalí, Hollywood film reflected popular fantasies and he celebrated the films of Buster Keaton and Harry Langdon ('one of the purest flowers of the screen and of our CIVILIZATION as well') over those of the avant-garde whose art is 'sublime, deliquescent, bitter, putrefied' (Dalí 1998: 8).

Several critics have noted that Batcheff's role recalls the conventional romantic roles of 1920s' cinema, in a form of self-parody of his own earlier film roles, such as the Russian officer in Raymond Bernard's *Le Joueur d'échecs / The Chess Player* (1927) or the sentimental hero of *La Sirène des tropiques*.[11] Batcheff's character is also clearly modelled on actors of popular American comedy, particularly the films of Harry Lloyd, Harry Langdon and above all Buster Keaton. In 1927 Buñuel had written an enthusiastic review of Keaton's *College* – 'as beautiful as a bathroom' (Hammond 2000: 61–2) – and the donkeys-and-pianos sequence quotes from the gag in *One Week* (1920) where Keaton tries to pull a piano into the house at the end of a long rope. (It also recalls *Poison* (1922), a play by the surrealist Roger Vitrac, where one of the characters pulls along a cable at the end of which a steamer has been attached). Similarly, in *The Paleface* (1922), a shot of Keaton kissing a girl is followed by the intertitle 'Two years later', followed by the same Keaton kissing the same girl, a sequence which is parodied in *Un chien andalou* where, as we saw, the intertitle 'Sixteen years earlier' is followed by the same actors, space and action as in the preceding shot. Matthew Gale notes that Batcheff's gesture of wiping away his mouth recalls Keaton's repeated gesture of wiping his eyes as a sign of disbelief in films such as *The Electric House* (1922) or *Sherlock Jr* (1924) (2007: 89). Moreover, the idea for the male cyclist recalls Lorca's short play *El paseo de Buster Keaton / Buster Keaton's Outing* (1925), in which an effeminate Keaton falls off his bicycle and has failed heterosexual encounters. Even the stripes may have migrated from the zebra-patterned stockings of Lorca's female character to the box and tie! (Gibson 1997:195–6) The character of the sexually ambiguous cyclist in his chambermaid costume meshes allusions to Keaton with a reference to Lorca's own homosexuality, and we saw that Lorca himself considered the mythical dog of the title as a reference to himself.

The enthusiasm for popular American comedy evident in Buñuel and Dalí is matched by their contempt for 1920s' European avant-garde film, notably abstract film and the Impressionist cinema.[12] They both claim *Un chien andalou* was produced as an aggressive reaction against avant-garde cinema. Buñuel declared that the film was 'deliberately anti-plastic, anti-artistic' (Mellen 1978: 151); while for Dalí, the film 'ruined in a single evening ten years of pseudo-intellectual post-war avant-gardism. That foul thing which is figuratively called abstract art fell at our feet, wounded to the death, never to rise again [...] There was no longer room in Europe for the little maniacal lozenges of Monsieur Mondrian' (Dalí 1968: 212). Several elements in the film can indeed be read as a parodic reworking of avant-garde films, although this aspect of the film does not seem to have been recognized in the critical reception. The focus on form among German abstract film directors (Richter, Eggeling, Ruttman), for instance, is pastiched in the formal rhyming of shapes like the diagonal stripes or the repeated circular motif, or in the poetic montage of dissolves from female armpit to sea urchin. Formal elements – the proliferation of diagonals and round shapes in script and film, for instance – displace and replace psychological realism. Moreover, the film appears to parody the aestheticism and focus on psychology and stylistic conventions of Impressionist directors such as Germaine Dulac, Abel Gance, Marcel L'Herbier or Jean Epstein. The sudden irrational changes of behaviour of the characters – the air of defiance then of compassion of the female character at the cyclist's fall, the authoritarian behaviour of the double switching to intense emotion when he hands over the books, the initial passivity of the female character which shifts without any transition to assertiveness in a later sequence – are a humorous take on the interest in psychological motivation among Impressionist film directors. The Impressionists' use of technical effects – rapid editing, dissolves, superimpositions, iris shots, high angle shots, close-ups – to express the subjective vision of the protagonists, is also exploited in *Un chien andalou* where they are exposed as cinematic tricks and used to disrupt, rather than facilitate, narrative continuity. The superimposition of the figure of the cyclist against the street appears unmotivated, for instance, as does the self-knotting tie. Emptied of meaning, these shots expose the arbitrary nature of the cinematic device (Thiher 1979: 31). The alternating shots of the female protagonist's face in medium close-up and the death-head moth in close-up recall Epstein's montage techniques. Moreover, several scenes pastiche sequences from Impressionist films. For example, the scene where the female character sits down next to the cyclist's fetish objects laid out on the bed quotes the scene in Epstein's *La Chute de la maison Usher* where Usher raises his dead wife from the tomb (Short 2002: 78).[13] The killing of the double can be considered a parodic reworking of a sequence in L'Herbier's *Feu Mathias Pascal*, in which the hero is confronted with his former self which he tries to kill (Thiher 1979: 31). Mathias' slow-motion advance on his adversary, indicating the fantasy status of the scene, is repeated in *Un chien andalou*, but this time quite gratuitously, thus exposing the mannerisms of Impressionist technical devices. Similarly, the use of Wagner for the soundtrack recalls Epstein's use of extracts from Wagner (as well as Schubert, Mozart and Beethoven) for *Mauprat*. Although Desnos' article 'Avant-Garde Cinema', written after the première of *Un chien andalou* and Man Ray's *Les Mystères du château du Dé*, contrasts these two films with those of Impressionist directors (Hammond 1978: 36–8), the relationship actually appears to be less a case of simple opposition than of ironic quotation.

Furthermore, *Un chien andalou* can be read not only as a parody of contemporary films, but as a pastiche of the dominant genre of 1920s' cinema, melodrama – an approach suggested by J.H. Matthews, for instance, when he refers to 'several disparaging allusions to the conventions of the silent movie drama, ridiculing its pantomime of passion and stylized gesture' (Matthews 1971: 86). In chapter 2 the narrative elements of the film were discussed in terms of the melodramatic genre: on the one hand, topoi such as the moonlit night, the gory crime, the severed limb, the monstrous moth; and on the other, stylistic conventions such as theatrical actions, heightened or primal emotions, and the pervasive focus on death, all familiar to cinema-goers of the 1920s.[14] The film also includes theatrical elements linked to blood and sensuality characteristic of Spanish melodrama (Buñuel's scenario *Caballeria Rusticana* (1927) was itself an earlier pastiche of Hispanic melodrama). Since hyperbole is a rhetorical device which characterizes melodrama, exaggerated gestures and expression are already inscribed in the genre. As a consequence it might be difficult to determine whether Buñuel and Dalí's treatment of the melodramatic mode is in itself parodic, hyperbolic to the second degree as it were. The proliferation of elements of the gothic tale – the gruesome crime, the severed hand, the monstrous insect, burying alive – are scattered throughout the film in a fragmented fashion, however, without cohering into a sustained narrative. Moreover, melodramatic elements are mixed with comic gags, thus undermining their import. For example the moonlit night setting is undercut through its link to Marinetti's futurist injunction against romantic images: 'Let's kill the moonlight!', here performed quite literally, thus suggesting that Buñuel and Dalí were indeed playfully pastiching the genre.

The attraction of the melodramatic genre for Buñuel and Dalí can be explained, to a certain extent, by the similarity between melodramatic and dream structures. As the dramatization of the return of the repressed, melodramatic structures simulate the mechanisms of dreamwork.[15] The melodramatic stage is analogous to the space of dream or fantasy: oneiric and melodramatic narratives are similar in the absence of causal relations between events; the interference of alternative narratives; the focus on detail; displacement (fragmented bodies) and condensation (repeated signs), elements which were discussed earlier as characteristic of the film's narrative. Moreover, according to Peter Brooks, 'melodrama and psychoanalysis represent the ambitious, Promethean sense-making systems which man has elaborated to recuperate meanings in the world' (Brooks 1976: 202). He thus considers melodrama and psychoanalysis as hermeneutic activities based on a similar model: restoring rational order to a society or psyche threatened with disruption. *Un chien andalou* problematizes the very possibility of such restoration of rational order by resorting to random fragments of dream and melodrama which cannot be retrieved to create a coherent narrative.

## Early cinema and fairground intertexts

The film has affinities not only with contemporary cinema and culture, but also with popular entertainment forms of the pre-war years. Buñuel's first experience of the cinema was at the age of eight at the Farrucini in Saragossa, a makeshift cinema with wooden benches and a tarpaulin roof. Films at the time, recounts Buñuel, were 'like the sideshow at a country fair' (Buñuel 1984: 31). Even during their Residencia days, Buñuel, Dalí and Lorca would often go to the fairground: a photograph from 1923 shows Lorca and Buñuel against the painted backdrop of a plane at the San Antonio de la Florida fair in Madrid.[16] *Un chien andalou* clearly draws elements from pre-war cinema, especially Louis Feuillade's crime series and the films of Georges Méliès, themselves informed by popular entertainment models of the end of the nineteenth century, in particular the fairground, magic theatre and vaudeville theatre.

Clear echoes can be perceived in *Un chien andalou* of the French film director Louis Feuillade's popular crime series *Fantômas* (1913–14), based on best-selling serial novels (or *feuilletons)* written by Pierre Souvestre and Marcel Allain. Inspired by the highly mediatized activities of the anarchist group the Bande à Bonnot, they featured Fantômas, 'Emperor of crime' and 'Lord of terror', whose multiple crimes appeared as unmotivated, carnivalesque actions against society. Fantômas always escapes his pursuers and, as the model of revolt, he represents the triumph of anarchy over social order. This figure was one of the anti-heroes who fascinated both the dadaists (he figures on Dada's genealogical tree 'Erutaréttil'), and the surrealists, who glorified criminals in contemporary court cases such as the Bande à Bonnot, the presumed serial killer Landru, the eighteen-year-old parricide Violette Nozières and the von Papin sisters (who murdered their employer). As 'the man of a thousand faces', Fantômas assumes ever-changing identities, a trait shared by the detective in charge of the cases, Inspector Juve, and the categories of victim and accomplice fluctuate. There is, furthermore, little concern with resolution and moral restitution. The focus is less on solving a mystery than on the succession of horrors, crimes and chases, the pleasure of the reader deriving from the forever changing elements of the story, 'a popular corollary to a surreal dream text'

(Walz 2000: 64). The narratives were largely improvized, fragmentary and incoherent, indeed their very absence of artistry attracted the surrealists. *Un chien andalou* can be seen to have a number of affinities with *Fantômas:* in the unmotivated crime which goes unpunished; the shifting identities of its hero; the incoherence of its narrative and the excesses and crudeness of its style. Furthermore, allusions to specific *Fantômas* episodes are evident, for example, in the theme of the severed hand (*La Main coupée*) and the house with identical rooms (*Juve contre Fantômas*).[17]

Chapter 2 explored the influence of the 'cinema of attractions' on the structure of *Un chien andalou*. Buñuel and Dalí also drew on a number of themes from the films of Georges Méliès and other early film directors.[18] For example, the opening sequence echoes the scene in *Voyage dans la lune / A Trip to the Moon* (1902) where a shell is fired from earth and pierces the eye of the moon, which appears magnified to colossal proportions. As in *Un chien andalou,* Méliès' moon is coded female. More important, as a replay of fairground performances, early cinema's film-as-spectacle often screens the film-maker himself, in the guise of the magician who controls and transforms reality. In particular, the male magician performing magical acts on a female subject belongs to the magic theatre and early cinema's repertoire. *L'Escamotage d'une dame chez Robert Houdin / The Vanishing Lady* (1896), for example, transposes magic theatre's substitution trick: the magician (played by Méliès himself) covers a seated female figure with a cloth, removes it to reveal a skeleton, which is covered again, to finally restore the woman. In the opening scene of *Un chien andalou* the trick film intertext is present with Buñuel himself in the role of magician-*cinéaste* and the female protagonist as his assistant. With its elaborate mise-en-scène, its frontal framing producing a deliberately theatrical effect, its gradual build-up of suspense (knife-sharpening, moon-slicing, eye-slashing), this sequence calls on the conventions of the magic theatre stage.[19] Elsewhere, the appropriation of popular entertainment codes in the close-up shots of female part-bodies, breasts or eyes, recalls images of the fairground female assistant sawn into pieces; while the transformation of body-parts – breasts dissolved to buttocks, underarm hair to sea-urchin – allude to the substitution tricks played out by the male magician on his female subjects. In a study of early cinema Lucy Fischer has argued that Méliès' films are informed by a latent discourse on sexual politics in which 'the male enacts a series of symbolic rituals in which he expresses numerous often-contradictory attitudes towards women'. She uncovers the ambivalence of these films, where 'the rhetoric of magic bespeaks a fear of the female': the male magician both exercizes his power over woman by cutting her up or conjuring her up or away, then reconstituting her through magic acts, thereby displacing his fear of her by dematerializing her while appropriating her procreative powers (Fischer 1979: 33). Elaborating on Fischer's analysis, Linda Williams has argued that Melies' films present a symbolic re-enactment, obsessively repeated, of mastery over the threat of gender difference, a re-enactment played out in the scenarios of dismemberment / reintegration, or disappearance / reappearance of the woman's body (Williams 1981a). Her analysis of *Un chien andalou*'s prologue, as discussed in chapter 2, similarly focuses on the sequence as a mise en scène of the fear of castration and the symbolic enactment of the denial of sexual difference.

Not only does the part played by Buñuel have close affinities with Méliès' own roles in his magical acts on stage and screen, but it can be linked to other forms of fairground entertainment, where the magician becomes a surgeon. A further intertext for the opening sequence can

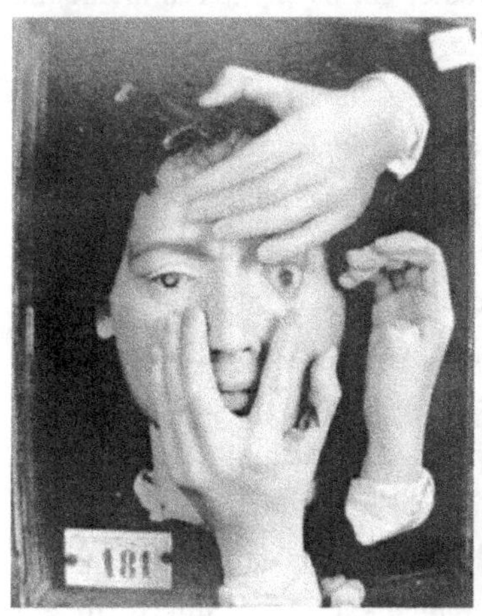


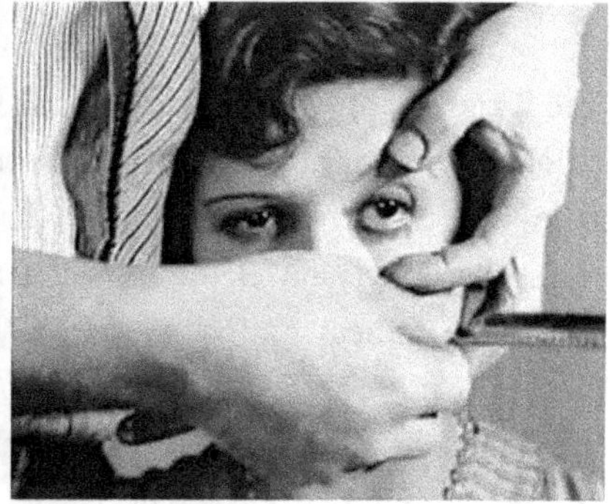

Nineteenth-century waxwork display of a cataract operation / Cutting the eye

be found in nineteenth-century fairground waxwork displays with their often gruesome presentations of physical ailments or operations – among which, of key significance, the waxwork of a cataract operation where two disembodied hands hold open the eye of a seemingly compliant woman which the doctor's scalpel prepares to pierce. This image, it seems, echoes a poem by Dalí, 'My girlfriend and the beach' (1927), quoted earlier in this chapter: 'My girlfriend loves the sleepy delicacy of toilets and the sweetness of lancet incisions on a curved pupil which is dilated for the extraction of a cataract' (Dalí 1998: 21).[20]

What is the effect of the appropriation of such fairground tricks and magical transgressions by Buñuel and Dalí? Does the parodic reworking of early cinematic codes and melodramatic structures in the film reinforce or subvert the patriarchal order of power and control? While *Un chien andalou* has been read as a resolutely radical, modernist (and indeed early postmodern) film, Buñuel and Dalí's return to images of the magic theatre of their childhood suggests that, even as they parody these outdated modes of spectacle, they play nostalgically with the magical fantasmagoric images of *fin-de-siècle* entertainment. *Un chien andalou* is, arguably, both radical and nostalgic. Like the magician-figure at the end of the nineteenth century who asserts his independence from industrialization, Buñuel and Dalí, I should like to argue, resort to outdated forms of entertainment and pastiche the material effects of early film in a regressive defense against 1920s' avant-garde modernity (abstract film). Against the realities of adulthood, they regress to infantile sexual fantasies: masturbatory sequences, gratuitous sadistic violence, Oedipal struggles against reified father-figures (the B-movie cop-dad who removes the son's feminine frills). Against the rationalization of postwar European society, they react by promoting the irrational, the arbitrary and the ludic. It was perhaps this nostalgic / regressive dimension of the film that the poet Jean Cocteau recognized when he commented: 'Hollywood was becoming a deluxe garage, and its films were more and more like sumptuous makes of automobiles. With *Un chien andalou* we were back to the bicycle' (quoted in Baxter 1994: 78).

The ambivalence of *Un chien andalou* is thus linked to the ambivalence of its intertextual processes. The foregoing analysis has shown that parody and pastiche are both a form of homage (for example to Buster

Keaton or Méliès) and critique (for example of Impressionist directors). The film draws on Hollywood comedy and melodrama ('anti-artistic film') on the one hand, experimental avant-garde film ('art-film') on the other. Yet it fits neatly into neither category. It occupies an ambivalent space: between cinematic conventions and their parodic reworking through the filter of characteristically surrealist images; and between modernity and nostalgia. This produces, for instance, scenes like that of the female protagonist expressing alarm at seeing the ants crawling out of the hand, a scene in which the conventions of psychological realism are exploited yet undercut by the incongruity of the image of the ants. Finally, we can conclude that the film is both radically modernist in its parodic use of conventional film techniques and avant-garde subversion, and apparently nostalgic in its engagement with popular prewar entertainment codes.

## Destabilizing gender roles

However, *Un chien andalou* was not only a playground for adolescent boys to indulge in playful antics. It was also a cruel reflection, through comedy, of an unstable age. The term 'perros andaluces', as we saw earlier, was used by Buñuel and his fellow-students to refer to a group of Andalusian poets at the Residencia and the film, according to Aranda, is an account of their 'infantilism, castration complex, sexual ambivalence, identity problems, etc., and their inner struggle to get rid of their bourgeois heritage in order to set the adult free' (Aranda 1975: 46). The reference goes beyond the Andalusian poets, however, and the film can be read in the wider context of the social and ideological situation of the post-war generation of young men and women. As Georges Sadoul observes: 'The surrealist *mal du siècle* was expressed in *Un chien andalou*, which is the image of an educated youth in a confused state of revolt. The sincerity of this great impotent cry of rage gave it a tragic humanity' (Sadoul 1949: 200). In what follows we will, consequently, situate the film in the 1920s' social and cultural context that informed the contradictions and tensions of identity and gender construction enacted in the film via the instabilities of male and female identities and relations.[21]

The effects of the 1914–1918 war, with its disfigured bodies and disturbed minds, brought about fundamental shifts throughout Europe in the ways in which the body was conceptualized and identity constructed.[22] While dominant discourses suppressed the traumatic images of dismemberment and dislocation in a political and artistic 'return to order', counterdiscourses (such as those of the dadaists and surrealists) privileged art forms which, on the contrary, exposed the violence done to the integral body or unified identity. They privileged images of the body as fragment, fetish or fantasy, and represented identity as indeterminate and fluid. The unstable images of male and female identities, and the representations of gender indifferentiation explored in their films should also be linked to the collapse of the nineteenth-century myth of the heroic individual (enacted in figures such as Chaplin and Keaton); to the growing demand among women for social and sexual emancipation; to the generalized feminization of society as a result of increasing consumerism, accompanied by the emergence of the (apparently contradictory) androgynous figure of the New Women. As a result, seemingly fixed definitions of masculinity and femininity gave way to fluid destabilizing models, theorized in the works of Freud or Havelock Ellis, in particular. As articulated in *Un chien andalou*, this disruption produces the male protagonists who embody conflicting models of masculinity: in the traditional image of the male dominator (Buñuel), the more ambivalent shifting masculinity of Batcheff in his roles of cyclist and double, and the homosexuality of the androgyne. Similarly, the contradictions and sudden shifts of the female protagonist project a model of femininity which reflects the shifting gender identities of interwar Europe. Let us look at these models more closely.

In the first place, the classic couple male torturer / female victim was explored in the last section as a stock image of early film melodrama. This choice of scenario has been linked to Buñuel's misogyny by Paul Julian Smith (1995), who argues that 'his films are a cavalcade of sexual violence against women', women who are fetishized, passive objects. Buñuel's choice of the actress Simone Mareuil to play the part of the female protagonist seems to confirm this misogynistic attitude: in a letter to Pepín Bello he expresses his regret that the latter could not be in Paris to play a role in the film and 'fuck the star, who's randy, full-bodied with big tits, imbecilic and not ugly' (Gibson 1997: 202). Beyond the personal and anecdotal, however, is a social context where traditional images of the male were also being questioned and challenged. If Buñuel allocates himself a clearly-defined sadistic role in the prologue, it is not sustained and his character is not developed; Dalí appears fleetingly, twice; the main protagonist shifts between cyclist, lover, child and superego; and in the closing shot the man on the beach is undifferentiable from the cyclist. Furthermore, the figure of the androgyne can be read as the fleeting object of the desire of the main protagonist who quickly displaces his desire from street to apartment, from male to female, disavowing his homosexual tendencies. Drawing on the in-depth analysis of Buñuel's films by Peter Evans (1995), Phil Powrie argues that the instability of the male protagonists is less a 'figuration of desire', as maintained by Williams (1981a), than 'a symptom of masculinity in crisis', an expression of male masochism (Powrie 1998: 162). The character demonstrates firstly a literal lack of stability: the cyclist comes off his bicycle, the double falls to his death. Secondly, he lacks stable contours (he has a hole in his hand), loses body parts (his mouth disappears) and acquires others, is conjoined with the animal (ants emerging from his flesh) or the female (female body hair growing on his face). Clearly, such limit-forms of corporeal representation constitute a radical revision of the classical body as whole and contained and, by extension, a revision of identity as fixed and immutable. Further, the male character is infantilized (childish clothes, onanism), fetishized (clothes and box on bed), feminized (frills, female body hair) and reified (objects washed up as flotsam). More conventionally, the male character pursues the object of his desire without success, he repeats the Oedipal scenario (primal scene, separation from the maternal figure, punishment by the father-figure), but romance is frustrated, oedipal conflict left unsolved, and sexual gratification constantly deferred. Mouth erased (in a lateral movement of the hand which echoes the action in the first sequence, but this time with an irreversible effect), face invaded by female body hair, he is, finally, reduced to a pitiable brutish state. Through such figures of destabilization – unstable contours or identity, desire unfulfilled, actions devoid of finality – the male self is projected as the decentred subject, a subject split, fragmented, displaced or dissolved in the other.

Desnos was one of the few to underline the unrelenting diagnosis operating in the film when he stated in 1929: 'One of the greatest qualities of such a film is to bring man face to face with himself, skinned and flayed, in a merciless autopsy' (Desnos 1992: 187). Read from such a perspective, it is significant that the character played by Batcheff has affinities, generally, with the roles played by Keaton and Chaplin in the tragi-comic portrayals of a conventional masculinity undermined and disorientated[23]; and, more specifically, with the character of the clergyman in Dulac's film *The Seashell and the Clergyman*.

Critical attention has thus focused almost exclusively on the misogyny (Buñuel) and, more recently, the ambivalence (Batcheff) of the male characters. The female protagonist, on the other hand, has mostly been reduced to victim of Buñuel's scalpel or object of Batcheff's desires. A first reading of *Un chien andalou* would appear to reinforce the misogynistic ideology encoded in *fin-de-siècle* entertainment of male domination and female submission – a reading supported by early feminist critiques of Surrealism as a deeply misogynistic movement dominated by men, where violation of the female body is played out as a defense against male castration fears (Gauthier 1971). This attitude is enacted in the prologue where the violent act is both sexual penetration and revenge on the woman who dares to look back. The stock melodramatic codes of male domination and female subjugation (eye-slitting scene), the image of woman as passive spectacle (frontal shots) or fetishized object (close-ups of part-bodies) for the active male gaze, can be seen to invite the narcissistic identification and scopophilic (fetishistic) pleasure of the (male) spectator.[24] Traditional tropes of femininity are indeed present: the female character is subjugated, depersonalized (headless, reduced to buttocks and breasts), fickle (she submits to the first man's gruesome act, rejects the second man's advances, and walks off with the third man), dissimulating (her disappearances and reappearances are unexplained), duplicitous (in the prologue she is both passive victim and willing accomplice, behaviour which conforms to contemporary psychological theories of woman's 'essential' duplicity and masochism[25]).

In this reading, *Un chien andalou* appears to reinforce traditional patriarchal attitudes on the level of both narrative and spectatorial position, and may lead one to conclude that Buñuel and Dalí were too close to the escapist topos of magic as a poetic means of transforming reality to radically challenge the social, moral and sexual conventions encoded in early fantasmagoria or trick film. Yet restricting the female character to the role of victim or object in this way is to ignore the complex, and often contradictory, explorations of gender identity. In fact, one critic has, at least, credited the female protagonist with an active role, summarizing the story as a young woman's struggles with three men (Demeure 1954). A second, less reductive, discourse on gender, latent yet quietly subverting the overt discourse, can also be detected. Like the male protagonists, the female protagonist is complex and ambivalent, marked by inconsequential behaviour and an ever-shifting identity. The traditional relation between male-oppressor and female-oppressed is undermined in the prologue itself in that she is the subject of the steady gaze, denying objectification under the magician / surgeon / film director's scalpel or the male spectator's voyeuristic gaze. Moreover, her role constantly shifts in the course of the narrative between maternal (expressing a motherly concern for the cyclist when he falls off his bicycle) and sexual (as object of Batcheff's sexual advances); between passive (calmly submitting to Buñuel's razor, reluctantly submitting to Batcheff's caresses, coyly submitting to her beach lover's reprimand) and active (defiantly asserting her physical integrity against Batcheff's loss of face, cavalierly rejecting him for a new lover on the beach). The frontiers of her body are repeatedly invaded or transformed by male actions: eye slit with a razor, breast and buttocks jumbled under the caress of the male, nomadic body hair, naked body literally dissolved when the male protagonist touches her back. Yet she miraculously survives Buñuel's scalpel or Batcheff's caresses, as if defying the role of object to which the male protagonists repeatedly strive to subject her. Hence while she appears naked in a meadow or disappears in a literal dissolve (at the hand of the dying male), she reappears, fully clothed, in the apartment. She moves from object to subject of desire: from domestic passivity, mirroring the self-absorbed image of the lacemaker, she shifts in one shot to the subject of publicly exposed sexual appetite when she passionately embraces the cyclist in the street. She moves from submitting to the transformation of body-parts under the caresses of

Batcheff to actively exchanging mouth, hair and tongue in the death-head moth scene. Asserting her aggressive phallic femininity – vigorously applying lipstick, twice defiantly sticking out her tongue – she turns her back on male number two, whose bodily integrity has been eroded. The woman's revolt is, however, shortlived: in the next sequence, when she meets a new lover on the beach, male domination is re-asserted via her coy submission – and final entrapment.[26]

The death-head moth sequence, in which hybrid bodies and shifting identities occupy a paradoxical space of play and anguish, can be interpreted as the sequence in which gender roles are most radically subverted. 'This hilarious sequence compresses an extraordinary range of sexual signifiers into a dance between genders', notes Dawn Ades (1995: 78). Body parts disappear (Batcheff wipes away his mouth) or migrate between the male and female protagonists (Batcheff acquires female hair and Mareuil a phallic tongue), recalling the optical tricks of the fun-fair, in particular the paradigm of the bearded lady or hermaphrodite. However, the sequence is also profoundly disturbing in its ambiguity. Shots and reverse shots structure this choreography, between woman and moth first, then between female and male. The eyeline matches and shots and counter-shots suggest it is the woman's intense gaze that conjures up first the death-head moth, then the man's presence in the apartment room, replicating the earlier sequence where the female character appears to conjure up the presence of the reconstituted male from his clothes (Talens 1993: 49). Through dissolves and iris-shots – cinematic strategies used here to suggest subjectivity – the moth turns to monster, while the shots and counter-shots link it, in a series of point-of-view shots, to both the male and female characters. As a result, the monster can be identified with the male protagonist's animal sexuality or the female's vampire nature. The exchanges between the couple are next played out as an exchange of body parts: the male loses his mouth, then acquires the female's body hair in its place, while the woman in reaction defiantly asserts her femininity by applying lipstick, as well as her own masculinity, by sticking out a phallic tongue, abandons her companion who has been literally defaced and feminized, to join another man on the beach, whose bodily integrity appears quite complete.

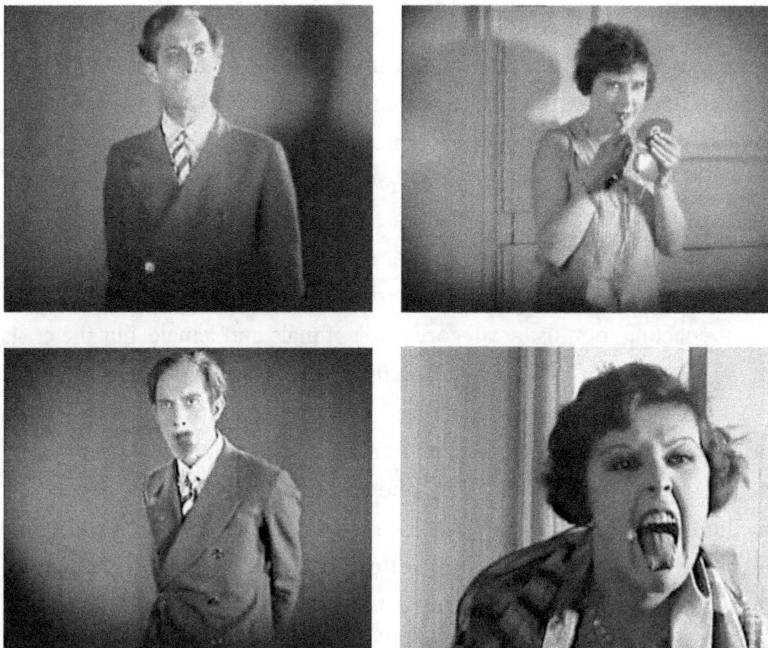

Migrating body-parts

This play on gender roles was not mentioned in the critical reception when the film was first shown. Yet the established principles of a stable, unified ego on the one hand, and of fixed notions of femininity and masculinity on the other, were being challenged in the 1920s in the writings of Freud, Weininger and Ulrichs, among others. The surrealists themselves rejected notions of identity as essentialist concept or ontological given, favouring instead a notion of identity as a mobile construct constantly remodelled by desire, as played out in this sequence. Far from being a closed entity, the body's comforting – or constraining – limits are constantly transgressed and extended.[27] The exchange of body parts between the male and female protagonists, however, produces less the surrealist resolution of opposites, as in the figure of the androgyne, or a collapse into the *informe* of gender indifferentiation, than an oscillation between male and female positions. This is actualized in a form of play where fixed gender codes are relaxed rather than renounced, not only (on the level of representation) in favour of fluctuating signs marking the shifting spaces of male and female signifiers, but also (on the level of the filmic text) as a more generalized eroticism created through the rhythmic movement of shot and counter-shot and the humorous scrambling of gender codes, in figures presenting an oscillatory movement rather than a blurring of distinctions. As a result, not only are fixed notions of femininity and masculinity disrupted, but the categories themselves are questioned, creating a 'third sex' which is neither male nor female. This can be linked to cross-dressing which, Marjorie Garber (1997: 17) argues, is a disruptive event enacting 'not just a category crisis of male and female, but the crisis of category itself'. Whether oscillating between male and female gender positions, or engaged in a generalized eroticism, the filmed body is the site of conflicting impulses articulated as duplication, multiplicity, fragmentation, impulses that both deny and exacerbate difference. The filmic medium is a privileged medium for staging such ambivalent and mobile identities in signifiers in continual flux, in the dissolves, diegetic disruptions or optical tricks which make bodies merge, multiply or disintegrate, reify or resuscitate, denying the stability of the body as a distinct(ive) unity. The disjunctive self is inscribed not only graphically through the images of the body transgressed, but also formally in the film syntax in montage techniques which make visible its wounds, grafts and cuts.

This discussion has explored the fluid remappings of identity and the body in the shifting, often perverse images of *Un chien andalou*. These unstable images problematize our reading of the filmic text. On the one hand, the couple composed of the male magician-cinéaste and his female victim appears to invite complicitous projections of the masculine gaze and combative protests by the feminist spectator. On the other hand, the disruptive strategies encoded in the film and the absence of a fixed spectatorial position disorient perception, and elicit a reading which disrupts the stable symbolic order. In her analysis of Georges Bataille's pornographic texts, Susan Sontag claims that they are transgressive, 'breaking through the level of consciousness', and hence emancipatory (1981: 28). Applying this notion to *Un chien andalou*, it can be argued that the visually and psychically shocking images of violation of the body (both body as representation and filmic body) are acts of liberation of the psyche from the constraints of bourgeois repression. Similarly, as Susan Rubin

Suleiman (1990: 146–50) has suggested in the context of Surrealism, perversions of the normative body can be considered as the rebellious actions of the son against paternal law, hence liberating. Such perversions are present both in the film's images of hybrid and fragmented bodies and in its parodic intertextual practices.

Finally, the antithetical readings to which the film lends itself – readings focusing on the dehumanization of the female figure expressing a misogynistic position, or on the perversion of normative gender roles liberating the viewer from repressive constraints – reflect the often contradictory positions of the surrealists themselves on the question of sexual issues. Their debates on sexuality in the late 1920s reveal complex and often antithetical attitudes towards gender relations: for example they passionately defend gender difference, while also seeking to collapse difference.[28] These positions, often tentatively formulated, reflect the ideological and cultural contradictions – in constructions of identity, self and other, masculinity and femininity – which were dominant in the 1920s, contradictions which were enacted in *Un chien andalou*.

## Notes

1 For an analysis of the film in the context of Spanish culture, see Morris (1972), Sánchez Vidal (1988).
2 Dalí's secondary education was at the Marist Brothers' College in Figueras.
3 For an analysis of the links between Buñuel and Dalí's texts and *Un chien andalou* see Finkelstein (1996).
4 See photograph of Buñuel in this role in Krohn (2005: 192).
5 For an analysis of the links between the Spanish avant-garde and Surrealism see Morris (1972).
6 Bazin's comment on Buñuel's third film, the documentary *Las Hurdes* (1932) could also be applied to *Un chien andalou*: 'Spanish tradition is combined in Buñuel with Surrealism. The taste for the horrific, the sense of cruelty, the search for extreme aspects of the human being, are inherited from Goya, Zurbaran and Ribera, the tragic sense of the human which these artists expressed in detail in their representations of the most extreme forms of human degeneration' (Bazin 1975: 76).
7 For an analysis of the eye in Surrealism see Eager (1961), Siegel (1982), Jay (1994).
8 For details of Buñuel's experience in the cinema in the 1920s, see Buñuel (1984: 87–103), Matthews (1971), Drummond (1977).
9 For details of Buñuel's experience in theatre production see Mimozo-Ruiz (1990).

10 For Sánchez-Vidal, this is the key text to an understanding of *Un chien andalou*. It was originally published by Buñuel, who was editor of the cinema rubric for *La Gaceta Literaria*, and whose view of the article is less positive. In a letter to Pepin Bello (8 November 1927), he writes: 'I can see all the bluffing behind his theories, and his desire to appear right up to date with his avant-gardism.' (Sánchez Vidal 1994: 193)
11 Abel (1984: 483), Aranda (1975: 37–8), Drummond (1977: 79), Powrie (1998: 162).
12 For an analysis of *Un chien andalou* as a critique of 1920s' avant-garde film directors see Thiher (1979), Short (2002), Fotiade (2006).
13 A similar scene occurs in Buñuel's *Tristana* (1970).
14 Topoi such as the death-head moth and the double are also present in Edgar Allen Poe's short tales 'The Go-Bug' and 'The Telltale'.
15 For a discussion of the links between melodramatic and dream structures see Brooks (1976), Williams (1991).
16 See *Buñuel 100 Years* (2000: 48).
17 Buñuel returned to the theme of Fantômas in *Le Phantôme de la liberté / The Phantom of Liberty* (1974) in which a man kills several people randomly in the street (in an echo of the surrealist act!), is sentenced to death, freed, and congratulated for his crime.
18 The close-up shots of the death-head moth can be linked to the magnified images of insects in Charles Urban's popular documentary series *Unseen World* (1903).
19 See also René Clair's *Entr'acte* where the corpse turns magician and conjures away the funeral procession; or the clergyman-(al)chemist in *La Coquille et le clergyman*, who conjures up the woman's head trapped in a vase. For a discussion of the fairground intertext in 1920s' dada and surrealst films, see Adamowicz (2001).
20 Joan M. Minguet Battlori links the opening scene to films of eye surgery by the ophthalmologist Ignacio Barraquer in Barcelona in 1917 (2003: 92–4).
21 This section develops the ideas explored in Adamowicz (2001).
22 For an excellent analysis of shifting gender roles in the interwar years in France see Roberts (1994).
23 Chaplin had a copy of the film, which had several screenings in his California house, and his description of some of the scenes terrified his daughter Geraldine. Yet he apparently had little liking for the film. 'It's just a stupid film', he is reported to have said to a female friend. (Baxter 1994: 116)
24 See Mulvey (1975).
25 See Walz (2000: 107).
26 The theme of repression and female inconstancy as a projection of the fear of woman is a recurrent feature of Buñuel's films: see for example *Ensayo de un Crimen/The Criminal Life of Archibaldo de la Cruz* (1955) and *Cet Obscur Objet du désir/That Obscure Object of Desire* (1977).
27 For an analysis of the shifting images of (self-)identity in Surrealism see Adamowicz (1998: 129–58).
28 See Pierre (1992).

# Conclusion

In November 1929 Buñuel was commissioned by the Vicomte de Noailles to make a seventeen-minute short with sound, as a birthday present for his wife Marie-Laure. While Buñuel and Dalí worked on the scenario together, this film, more than *Un chien andalou*, is the expression not so much of individual authorship than of the collective voice of the surrealist group (Hammond 1997: 42). Initially planned as a sequel to *Un chien andalou*, it was titled *La bestia andaluza* / *La bête andalouse* on the shooting script, then changed to *Abajo la Constitucion!*, and finally *La edad de oro* / *L'Age d'or*, and developed into a 60-minute feature. There are echoes of *Un chien andalou* in its narrative disjunctions, disruptive images and forceful social critique. The scope of *L'Age d'or* is much broader, however: for Linda Williams the film 'is a questioning of society and of the illusory unity of the social body, once more through the disruptive force of erotic desire' (1981a: 131). The scandal, so desired for *Un chien andalou*, exploded at one of the early screenings of *L'Age d'or* at Studio 28 in November 1930. The cinema was attacked by extreme right groups, the Anti-Jewish League and the Patriotic League, who threw smoke-bombs, smashed up the seats, hurled ink at the screen, and destroyed the surrealist exhibits in the foyer. The Chief of Police Chiappe denounced the film as *filth* (*ordure*) and had all copies of the film confiscated, because it allegedly disturbed public order. As a consequence it was banned in France until 1981. The reputation of *Un chien andalou* certainly profited from the scandal of *L'Age d'or*, which rebounded on the earlier film, to the point where some commentators (for example Cyril Connolly, cited in chapter 1) confused the first screening of the two films.

Chapter 2 argued that in *Un chien andalou* there is a convergence of a number of motifs and aesthetic processes which were already present not only in Dalí and Buñuel's texts and paintings, but also in the wider context of the Spanish and Paris avant-gardes. The film can therefore be read as a collective production, a crossroads, a point of intersection voicing a community of discourses in which the visions, obsessions and anxieties of a group and a period meet and intermingle. The film in its turn generated further developments not only in Dalí and Buñuel's later works, but also among the surrealist group itself, and avant-garde and mainstream film directors.

Dalí's 1930s' paintings echo the iconography of *Un chien andalou* in their portrayal of rotting donkeys and ant-infested flesh, severed hands, cyclists and grand pianos, superimposed and double images, as for example in *William Tell* (1930), *Babaouo* (1932), *The Invisible Man* (1933) or *Autumn Cannibalism* (1936–37). He worked on other scenarios and screenplays which were never filmed, such as *Babaouo* (1932), and *The Surrealist Woman* (1937) for the Marx Brothers. He designed the set for the dream sequence of Hitchcock's *Spellbound* (1945), in which a woman with giant scissors cuts up heavy drapes covered with giant eyes. The following year, he collaborated with Walt Disney on an animated film *Destino*. They spent eight months in the film studios working on this project, which was abandoned for financial reasons (it was completed and released in 2004). It presents Dalí's familiar repertory of images, including naked cyclists, swans turning into elephants then pyramids, and eye and sea-urchin superimposed.[1]

Buñuel became one of Europe's leading film directors, producing a total of thirty-one films. There are direct quotations from his first film, as well as more general affinities, throughout his film production. In *Las Hurdes / Land without Bread* (1933), a 27-minute documentary about an Asturian village, the image of the carcass of the donkey being devoured by bees is considered by Bazin as far more striking than the sequence of donkeys on pianos (1975: 69). Edwards, following Kyrou, sees this film as completing Buñuel's 'surrealist trilogy', produced in a spirit of revolt (2004: 80). His Mexican films quote images from *Un chien andalou*, such as hand and razor (*Robinson Crusoe* 1952), tie and diagonally striped box (*The Young One* 1954), or female inconstancy (*The Criminal Life of Archibaldo de la Cruz* 1955). His European films are also full of references to specific images from *Un chien andalou*: in *The Discreet Charm of the Bourgeoisie* (1972), for example, a grand piano swarming with red insects is used as a torture instrument for student militants; and in the scene at the end of *That Obscure Object of Desire* (1977), a seamstress seated in a shop-window, mending a slit in a piece of cloth, recalls the image of *The Lacemaker* in the earlier film. However, more important than such isolated iconographic echoes are more substantial characteristics of the films which found their original expression in the 1929 film: the shifts between fantasy and reality, the anarchic energy, the satirical assault on bourgeois society, which both scandalized and entertained the bourgeoisie.

It is difficult to determine the film's impact on later cinema, whether avant-garde, experimental or mainstream films. Indeed, since it has been argued in this study that *Un chien andalou* is as much a collective production as the creation of two individuals, it would seem to be vain to isolate the film's direct influence from that of surrealist iconography, 1920s' cinema, or popular entertainment codes, which converge in the film. For Buñuel himself, films such as Georges Hugnet's *La Perle* and Michel Gorel's *Bateaux parisiens*, both from 1929, were made in the same spirit as *Un chien andalou* (Aranda 1975: 58), hence sharing a cultural ambience. The postwar generation of surrealist film directors – Jan Svankmajer, Nelly Kaplan, Alejandro Jodorovsky – have acknowledged their debt to the film, and Surrealism in general, while extending (and questioning) the parameters of what constitutes a 'surrealist film'. Beyond the small repertory of surrealist film directors, a large number of films echo and extend *Un chien andalou*: for example Maya Deren's *Meshes of the afternoon* (1943), Hitchcock's *Vertigo* (1958), Jean-Jacques Beineix's *37.2 le matin / Betty Blue* (1976), James Cameron's *The Terminator* (1984), Almodovar's *Matador* (1986) or David Lynch's *Blue Velvet* (1986), among many others.[2]

Eighty years later, what is still radical in a film claimed to be 'a desperate, passionate call to murder'? Can *Un chien andalou* still be considered a revolutionary film in the twenty-first century? When Breton admitted to Buñuel in 1955: 'It's sad, *mon cher* Luis [...] but it's no longer possible to scandalize anybody!' (Buñuel 1984: 114), he was referring to culture's capacity to retrieve for the mainstream what initially appears scandalous. Yet critics have continued to focus on the film's radical impact. For Walker (1976), *Un chien andalou* and *L'Age d'or* 'remain the only art films to change the way most of us see and think about cinema. They are the only avant-garde productions by artists, in more than a century of cinema, that have seriously impinged on the mainstream.' And when a new print of the film was released in 2004, reviews were positive about its continuing transformative potential.[3]

The body has been banalized in postmodern anatomical displays of the medieval image of the body hanged, drawn and quartered. Taboos have been raised, whether the taboo of the sanctity of the whole body when we look back, or of the body as destiny, when we look forward to science's seemingly endless capacity to reshape the body. In our culture of clips and soundbites which has adopted the eye-slicing image as the paradigmatic model of filmic violence and sadism; where fast splicing and cutting have become cinematic conventions; where the uncanny underside of the real is a stock recipe of horror films and B-movies; where pastiche is an amateur pastime and the postmodern greedily retrieves all disruptions; in such a culture, can the film continue to shock and disturb its audiences? Does the repetition of eye-slitting scenes, from *The Terminator* to *The Phantom of the Opera*, have the effect of desensitizing the viewer to their traumatic impact, whence the need for a continuing escalation of shock images to reactivate the trauma? Even the dissected eye is no longer a taboo, and we rarely flinch at seeing it being cut into. Contemporary artists have cut open and explored all body parts – whether by dissection (Damien Hirst), endoscopy (Mona Hatoum) or surgical operations (Orlan). Images of bodies dissected are now a commonplace on our TV screens, to be relished within the comfort of our domestic space. Hospital series, forensic series and programmes on aesthetic surgery are not transgressive: they are produced and viewed in morally approved contexts – health, beauty, justice – and in socially accepted environments, inducing the feel-good factor, not shock. The viewer is prepared for the encounters on this dissecting table. Operations and dissections are carefully framed and justified within the narrative, humanized and instrumentalized, so that nothing is unexpected. What does that leave for the arch-criminal or the sexual deviant in a society where they are often recuperated as heroes, whether Jack the Ripper's violent cut-and-slash crimes or Sweeney Todd's aestheticized dissection of corpses? In *Un chien andalou*, by contrast, we are unprepared for the opening scene, which is disconnected from any diegetic development, underscoring the gratuity of the violence of Buñuel's surgical slash. The opening sequence in the film, far from being instrumentalized and recuperable, is an end in itself. There is no frame, no context, to fall back on: we are faced with the full indigestible horror of the image in its material presence. The ambivalent position of the viewer – as detective (or his avatars, psychoanalyst or film critic) or dreamer, as victim or aggressor, Inspector Juve or Fantômas – cannot finally be resolved. And although the careful mending of the ripped cloth by the seamstress in *That Obscure Object of Desire* has been interpreted as Buñuel in his last film closing the wound opened in his first (Carrière); although the public's acclaim of the murderer in *The Phantom of Liberty* has been read as an example of recuperation of Buñuel's 'passionate call to murder' (Richardson 2006: 43), the opening sequence remains irretrievable. *Un chien andalou* continues to resist totalizing readings and to exert a fascination which no critical discourse can fully contain.

## Notes

1 An exhibition at Tate Modern, *Dalí & Film*, curated by Matthew Gale, explored the relations between Dalí's filmic and pictorial production; see Gale (2007).

2 See Richardson (2006) for a spirited analysis of the links between Surrealism and film.

3 See for example Jones (2004).

# Appendix 1: Synopsis

Music: tango.
Credits.
Intertitle: 'Once upon a time'.
A man stands at a window, sharpens a razor blade and tests it on his thumbnail. He opens a French-window, steps out onto a balcony, leans against the railing and looks up at the full moon. He stands behind a seated woman. The man holds her left eye open with thumb and index finger. A thin cloud passes over the moon. The razor blade slices the woman's eye.
Music: Wagner.
Intertitle: 'Eight years later'.
A young man rides a bicycle down a deserted Paris street. He is wearing a dark suit and white frills on his head, shoulders and hips. A striped box hangs on a strap round his neck. The young woman (with eye restored) sits reading in a bedroom. She looks up startled. The cyclist is still riding down the street. The woman throws down the book which falls open a a reproduction of Vermeer's *The Lacemaker*. The woman goes to the window and observes the cyclist who comes to a stop and falls over onto the road. She appears to mutter angrily. She rushes into the street, kneels beside the cyclist and kisses him passionately. She opens the box with a key and takes out a diagonally striped packet. The woman is back in the room, opens the box, and from their wrappings takes out a black tie and stiff collar. She replaces the black tie with a diagonally striped tie taken from the box, and carefully lays out tie and collar on the bed with the white frills. She sits beside the bed and stares at the items laid out. The tie ties itself twice, first quickly, then slowly.The woman turns her head and sees the cyclist staring at his hand. Ants swarm out of a hole in his palm. The woman goes up to the man and looks at the hand. The image of the ants dissolves into a woman's armpit, then a sea urchin in the sand, then a young androgynous person prodding with a stick a dismembered hand

lying on the road, in the middle of a crowd of people. The man and woman observe the scene from an upstairs window with increasing excitement. A policeman picks up the hand, puts it in a striped box, which he gives to the androgyne, and disperses the crowd. The androgyne stands in the middle of the street holding the box to her / his chest, and is run over by a car.
Music: Wagner then tango.
The man looks at the woman with overt sexual desire, approaches her, she draws back, he caresses her alternately clothed then naked breasts. The man drools, his eyes rolled upwards. The man again caresses the breasts, which dissolve into bare buttocks. The woman pushes the man away and retreats. The cyclist chases her round the room. She threatens him with a tennis racket hanging on the wall. The man looks round and grabs the end of two ropes. He pulls on the ropes and drags along two pieces of cork, two grand pianos with the rotting carcasses of donkeys lying over them, and two Marist priests lying on their backs. The woman opens the door and exits into an identical room. She closes the door on the cyclist whose hand, still ant-infested, is caught in the door. The woman looks round and sees the cyclist on the bed dressed in frills, with the striped box round his neck.
Intertitle: 'Towards three in the morning'.
Another man rings the doorbell (a waiter's hands shake a cocktail shaker), enters the room, goes up to the bed and orders the cyclist to get up, pulls off his frills, and throws them out of the window. He makes the cyclist stand facing the wall with his arms stretched out.
Music: Wagner.
Intertitle: 'Sixteen years earlier'.
The cyclist still stands facing the wall, the second man turns round (he is the cyclist's double) and advances slowly. He picks up two books from a school desk, clasps them to his chest, then hands them to the cyclist. As the second man walks away, the cyclist scowls, and the books turn into revolvers with which he shoots the second man in the back. The dying man begins his slow fall in the room, then in a park, clutching the back of a naked woman. The woman's image disappears. Four men come up, examine the body and carry it away in a procession.
Music: tango.
The woman enters the room and stares at the opposite wall. A dark mark on the wall dissolves into a death-head moth. A close-up reveals the skull shape. The cyclist appears in the room, covers his mouth with his hand. When he pulls his hand away, his mouth has disappeared. The woman

vigorously puts on lipstick. A clump of hair appears in place of his mouth. She checks her armpit, which is shaved. She sticks her tongue out at him, exits the room, and walks straight onto a beach. The breeze blows her hair, she waves to someone off-screen. A man on the beach dressed in golf clothes turns towards her. She runs up to him. He shows her his watch, which she pushes aside. She kisses him and they stroll along the pebble beach arm in arm. The man kicks out of the way the striped box washed up by the tide, while the woman picks up the cyclists' clothes and cord and gives them to the man, who throws them away as well. The couple walk on.
Intertitle: 'In the spring'.
A man and the woman are buried to their waist in sand, blinded and covered with insects.

# Appendix 2: Credits

Producer: Luis Buñuel
Script: Luis Buñuel and Salvador Dalí
Director: Luis Buñuel and Salvador Dalí
Assistant director: Pierre Batcheff
Music: *Liebestod* from Richard Wagner's *Tristan und Isolde*, two Argentinian tangos
Photography: Albert Duverger
Production manager: Marral
Sets: Pierre Schildknecht
Editing: Luis Buñuel
Cast: Simone Mareuil (the woman), Pierre Batcheff (the man), Luis Buñuel (man with razor), Salvador Dalí, Marral, and Jaime Miravilles (Marist priests), Fano Messan (androgyne), Robert Hommet (man on beach)
Running time: 16' 14"
Length: 430 metres
First screening: 6 June 1929, Studio des Ursulines, Paris
Original titles: *La Marista en la Ballesta / The Marist Sister with the Crossbow, Dangereux de se pencher en dedans / It's dangerous to lean inside*
Distribution: Les Grands Films Classiques (Paris)
Silent film in black and white

Video:
Les Grands Films classiques (1960) with added soundtrack
Connaisseur Videos (1994)

DVD:
Filmoteca Española (2003), restored by Ferrán Alberich at 16 frames a second (24 minutes)
BFI (2004) with introduction and commentary by Robert Short
Éditions Montparnasse (2005) with interviews with Philippe Rouyer, Dominique Rabourdin, Luis Buñuel, Jean-Claude Carrière.

# Appendix 3: Selected bibliography

## Screenplay

In French:

*La Révolution surréaliste* 12 (December 1929), 34–7.

*La Revue du cinéma* 1, 5 (November 1929), 3–16, trans. Maxime Zvoinski.

*Premier Plan* 13 (October 1961); *L'Avant-scène du cinéma* 27–8 (June–July 1963).

In English:

*'L'Age d'or' and 'Un chien andalou'*, trans. Marianne Alexander (Letchworth: Lorrimer Publishing, 1968).

*Un chien andalou*, Introduction Philip Drummond, Foreword Jean Vigo (London: Faber 1994)

## Critical sources

Abel, Richard (1984). *French Cinema. The First Wave, 1915–1929* (Princeton University Press).

Abel, Richard (1988). *French Film Theory and Criticism: A History / Anthology. Volume I 1907–1939* (Princeton University Press).

Adamowicz, Elza (1998). *Surrealist Collage in Text and Image. Dissecting the Exquisite Corpse* (Cambridge University Press).

Adamowicz, Elza (2001). 'Bodies Cut and Dissolved: Dada and Surrealist Film', in Alex Hughes and James S. Williams, eds., *Gender and French Cinema* (Oxford and New York: Berg), 19–33.

Ades, Dawn (1982). *Dali* (London: Thames & Hudson).

Ades, Dawn (1995). 'Surrealism: Fetishism's Job', in Anthony Shelton, ed., *Fetishism: Visualising Power and Desire* (London: Lund Humphries), 67–87.

Antheil, George (1945). *Bad Boy of Music* (New York: Doubleday).

Aranda, Juan Francisco (1975). *Luis Buñuel: A Critical Biography* (New York: Da Capo Press).

Aron, Robert (1929). 'Films de révolte', *La Revue du cinéma* 1(5): 41–5; trans. 'Films of Revolt', in Abel (1988: 432–6).

Artigas, Pere (1929). 'Un fil d'en Dalí', *Mirador* (Barcelona) (23 May).

Aub, Max (1991). *Luis Buñuel. Entretiens avec Max Aub* (Paris: Belfond).

Bataille, Georges (1985). *Visions of Excess. Selected Writings, 1927–1939* (Minneapolis: University of Minnesota Press).

Baxter, John (1994). *Luis Buñuel: A Biography* (London: Fourth Estate).

Bazin, André (1975). *Le Cinéma de la cruauté. De Buñuel à Hitchcock* (Paris: Flammarion).
Blakeston, Oswell [O.B.] (1929). 'Paris Shorts and Longs', *Close Up* (August), 143–4.
Bonitzer, Pascal (1971). 'Le Gros Orteil', *Cahiers du cinéma* 232: 14–23.
Bouissounouse, J. (1929). 'Dans la salle. Quand le public rit', *La Revue du cinéma* 1(5): 73–5.
Breton, André (1972). *Manifestoes of Surrealism*, trans. Richard Seaver and Helen R. Lane (University of Michigan Press).
Brooks, Peter (1976). *The Melodramatic Imagination. Balzac, Henry James, Melodrama, and the Mode of Excess* (New York and London: Yale University Press).
Brunius, Jacques Brunius (1929). '*Un chien andalou.* Film par Louis (sic) Buñuel', *Cahiers d'art* 4(5): 230–1.
Buñuel, Luis (1929). Preface to screenplay, *La Révolution surréaliste* 12: 34.
Buñuel, Luis (1958). 'The Cinema, Instrument of Poetry', in Hammond (2000: 112–6).
Buñuel, Luis (1978). 'Notes on the making of *Un chien andalou*' [1947], in Mellen (1978: 151–7).
*Buñuel, 100 Years / 100 Años. It's Dangerous to Look Inside / Es peligroso asomarse al interior* (2000) (New York: Instituto Cervantes / MOMA).
Buñuel, Luis (1984). *My Last Sigh* (London: Vintage Books).
Buñuel, Luis (2000). *An Unspeakable Betrayal. Selected Writings of Luis Buñuel* (Berkeley, Los Angeles, London: University of California Press).
Caws, Mary Ann (1981). 'Eye and Film: Buñuel's Act', in *The Eye in the Text. Essays on Perception, Mannerist to Modern* (Princeton University Press), 135–44.
Cesarman, Fernando (1982). *L'Oeil de Buñuel* (Paris: Éditions du Dauphin).
Comtesse de Beaumont (1929). 'Films européens', *Gringoire* (18 October).
Dalí, Salvador (1968). *The Secret Life of Salvador Dalí* [1942] (London: Vision).
Dalí, Salvador (1976). *The Unspeakable Confessions of Salvador Dalí* (London: W.H. Allen).
Dalí, Salvador (1998). *Oui. The Paranoid-Critical Revolution. Writings 1927–1933 by Salvador Dalí* (Boston: Exact Change).
Delons, André (1929). '*Un chien andalou.* Film de Buñuel', *Variétés* (Brussels) (15 July), 222.
Demeure, Jacques (1954). 'Luis Buñuel' – poète de la cruauté', *Positif* 2(10): 41–4.
Desnos, Robert (1929a). *'Un chien andalou'*, *Le Merle* 11 (28 June); in Desnos (1992: 186–7).
Desnos, Robert (1929b). 'Cinéma d'avant-garde', *Documents* 7, 385–7; trans. Paul Hammond (1978: 36–8).
Desnos, Robert (1992). *Les Rayons et les ombres* (Paris: Gallimard).
Drouzy, Maurice (1978). *Luis Buñuel. Architecte du rêve* (Paris: L'Herminier).
Drummond, Phillip (1977). 'Textual Space in *Un chien andalou*', *Screen* 18(3): 55–119.
Drummond, Phillip (1994). 'Surrealism and *Un chien andalou*', in Buñuel and Dalí (1994: v–xxiii).
Drummond, Phillip (2004). 'Domains of Cinematic Discourse in Buñuel's and Dalí's *Un chien andalou*', in Santaolalla et al. (2004: 101–10).

Dubois, Philippe and Edouard Arnoldy (1993). '*Un chien andalou*'. *Lectures et relectures, Revue belge du cinéma* 33–35.

Durgnat, Raymond (1967). *Luis Buñuel* (London: Studio Vista).

Eburne, Jonathan P. (2008). *Surrealism and the Art of Crime* (Ithaca, NY: Cornell University Press).

Edwards, Gwynne (1981). 'Lorca and Buñuel: *Asi que pasen cinco anos* and *Un chien andalou*', *Garcia Lorca Review* 9(2): 128–43.

Edwards, Gwynne (1982). *The Discreet Art of Luis Buñuel: A Reading of His Films* (London: Marion Boyars).

Edwards, Gwynne (2004). 'Luis Buñuel: The Surrealist Triptych', in Havard (2004: 79–95).

Eager, Gerald (1961). 'The Missing and Mutilated Eye in Contemporary Art', *The Journal of Aesthetics and Art Criticism* 20(1): 49–59.

Eisenstein, Sergei (1988). *Writings 1922–1934* (London: BFI).

Elsaesser, Thomas, ed. (1990). *Early Cinema: Space, Frame, Narrative* (London: BFI).

Epstein, Jean (1922). 'Freud, ou le nic-cartérianisme en psychologie', *L'Esprit nouveau* 16: 1864.

Evans, Peter W. (1995). *The Films of Luis Buñuel. Subjectivity and Desire* (Oxford: Clarendon Press).

Evans, Peter W., and Isabel Santaolalla, eds. (2004). *Luis Buñuel. New Readings* (London: BFI).

Everett, Wendy (1998). 'Screen as Threshold: The Disorienting Topographies of Surrealist Film', *Screen* 39(2): 141–52.

Ezra, Elizabeth (2000). *Georges Méliès* (Manchester University Press).

Farges, Joël (1975). 'L'image d'un corps', *Communications* 23.

Fieschi, Jean André (1972). 'L'Oeil tranche (notes sur le cinéma de Luis Buñuel)', *La Nouvelle Critique* 57(238): 78–84; in Dubois (1993: 181–5).

Finkelstein, Haim (1996). 'Dalí and *Un chien andalou*: the nature of a collaboration', in Kuenzli (1996: 128–41).

Fischer, Lucy (1979). 'The Lady Vanishes: Women, Magic and the Movies', *Film Quarterly* 33(1): 30–40.

Flitterman-Lewis, Sandy. 'The Image and the Spark: Dulac and Artaud Reviewed', in Kuenzli (1996: 110–26).

Fotiade, Ramona (1995). 'The Untamed Eye: Surrealism and Film Theory', *Screen* 36(4): 394–407.

Fotiade, Ramona (2006). '*Un chien andalou*. Luis Buñuel and Salvador Dalí, France, 1929', in Phil Powrie, ed., *The Cinema of France* (London, New York: Wallflower Press), 21–9.

Gale, Matthew, ed. (2007). *Dalí & Film* (London: Tate Publishing).

Garber, Marjorie (1997). *Vested Interests* (New York: Routledge).

Gauthier, Xavière (1971). *Surréalisme et sexualité* (Paris: Gallimard).

Ghéon, Henri (1929). 'Le film qui n'ose pas dire son nom: *Un chien andalou*', *Latinité* (December).

Gibson, Ian (1997). *The Shameful Life of Salvador Dalí* (London: Faber & Faber).

Goudal, Jean (1925). 'Surréalisme et cinéma', *La Revue hebdomadaire* (February), 343–57; trans. Hammond (1978: 49–56).

Grieveson, Lee, and Peter Krämer, eds. (2004). *The Silent Cinema Reader* (London and New York: Routledge).

Gunning, Tom (1989). 'An Aesthetic of Astonishment: Early Film and the (In)Credulous Spectator', *Art and Text* 34; in Williams (1995: 114–33).

Gunning, Tom (1990). 'The Cinema of Attractions: Early Film, Its Spectator and the Avant Garde', in Elsaesser (1990: 56–62).

Gunning, Tom (2004). ' "Now you see it now you don't". The temporality of the cinema of attractions', in Grieveson and Krämer (2004: 41–50).

Hammond, Paul (1974). *Marvellous Méliès* (London: Gordon Fraser).

Hammond, Paul, ed. (1978). *The Shadow and its Shadow: Surrealist Writings on Cinema*, first edition (London: British Film Institute).

Hammond, Paul (1997). *L'Age d'or* (London: BFI Classics).

Hammond, Paul, ed. (2000). *The Shadow and its Shadow: Surrealist Writings on the Cinema*, third edition (San Francisco: City Light Books).

Hansen, Miriam (1993). 'Early Cinema, Later Cinema: Transformations of the Public Sphere', *Screen* 34(3): 197–210; (adapted) in Williams (1995: 134–52).

Harris, Derek, ed. (1995). *The Spanish Avant-Garde* (Manchester University Press).

Havard, Robert, ed. (2004). *A Companion to Spanish Surrealism* (London: Tamesis).

Heymann, Claude (1930). 'Films sadiques', *L'Homme* (Marseille) (February).

Hugnet, Georges (1931). 'Joan Miró ou l'enfance de l'art', *Cahiers d'art* 6: 7–8.

Iampolski, Mikhail (1993). 'The Surrealist film and cinematic poetics: the case of *Un chien andalou*', in Thomas W. Gaehtgens, ed., *Künstlerischer Austausch. Artistic Exchange* vol III (Berlin: Akademie Verlad), 179–92.

Isnard, Daniel (1930). 'Les tendances morbides du film d'avant-garde', *Vasco* (Marseille) (7 January).

Jay, Martin (1993). *Downcast Eyes: The Denigration of Vision in Twentieth-Century French Thought* (Berkeley, Los Angeles, London: University of California Press).

Jones, Jonathan (2004). 'The Joy of Gore', *The Guardian* (7 February).

Krohn, Bill and Paul Duncan, eds. (2005). *Luis Buñuel. The Complete Films* (Cologne: Taschen).

Kuenzli, Rudolf E., ed. (1996). *Dada and Surrealist Film* (Cambridge Mass., London: MIT Press).

Kyrou, Ado (1962). *Luis Buñuel* (Paris: Seghers, Cinéma d'aujourd'hui).

Kyrou, Ado (1963). *Le Surréalisme au cinéma* (Paris: Le Terrain Vague).

Leiris, Michel (1992). *C'est-à-dire* (Paris: Jean-Michel Place).

Lenauer, Jean (1929). 'Deux nouveaux films: *Le Mystère du château du Dé* et *Un chien andalou*', *Pour vous. L'hebdomadaire du cinéma* (13 June), 4.

Liebman, Stuart (1996). '*Un chien andalou*: the talking cure', in Kuenzli (1996: 143–58).

Mabire, Jean-Marie (1962). 'Buñuel et le surréalisme', *Etudes cinématographiques* 20–21: 59–64.

Mabire, Jean-Marie (1965). 'Entretiens avec Philippe Soupault ', *Surréalisme et cinéma, Etudes cinématographiques* 38–39.

Marie, Michel (1981). 'Le Rasoir et la lune (sur le prologue d'*Un chien andalou*)', in Dominique Château, Andre Gardiès and François Jost, eds., *Cinémas de la modernité. Films, théories* (Paris: Klincksieck), 187–98; in Dubois (1993: 43–6).

Masoliver, Joan Ramon (1929). '*Un chien andalou* (film de Luis Buñuel i Salvador Dalí)', *Helix* 7: 7 (November).

Matthews, J.H. (1971). *Surrealism and Film* (University of Michigan Press).

Mellen, Joan, ed. (1978). *The World of Luis Buñuel: Essays in Criticism* (New York: Oxford University Press).

Mimozo-Ruiz, Duarte (1990). 'Théâtre et cinéma dans l'oeuvre de Luis Buñuel: d'*Hamlet* (1927) à *L'Age d'or* (1930)', in *Théâtre et cinéma années vingt. Une quête de la modernité* vol II (L'Age d'Homme), 52–71.

Mondragon (1949). 'Comment j'ai compris *Un chien andalou*', *Revue du Ciné-Club* 8–9 (May–June).

Montes, Eugenio (1929). '*Un chien andalou*', *La Gaceta Literaria* (15 June).

Morris, C.B. (1972). *Surrealism and Spain 1920–1936* (Cambridge University Press).

Moussinac, Léon (1929). 'Sur trois films dits d'avant-garde', *L'Humanité* (6 octobre), 4.

Mulvey, Laura (1975). 'Visual Pleasure and Narrative Cinema', *Screen* 16(3): 6–18.

Murcia, Claude (1994). '*Un chien andalou*'. '*L'âge d'or*'. *Étude critique* (Paris: Nathan).

Oswald, Laura (1981). 'Figure / Discourse: Configurations of Desire in *Un chien andalou*', *Semiotica* 33(1–2): 105–22.

Pastor, Brigida (2004). 'Luis Buñuel: el discurso subversivo en *Un chien andalou*', in Santaolalla et al. (2004: 355–67).

Peisson, Edouard (1931). '*Un chien andalou*', *Nouvel Age* 1: 85–6.

Benjamin Péret (1927). 'Les Odeurs de l'amour', in *Le Grand Jeu, Oeuvres complètes* I (Paris: Eric Losfeld 1969), 167.

Péret, Benjamin (1952). 'L'oeuvre cruelle et révoltée de Luis Buñuel', *Arts* 374; in *Oeuvres complètes* 6 (Paris: José Corti, 1992), 275–9.

Pérez, Gilberto (2004). 'The sliced eye and the primal scene identification and interpretation in *Un chien andalou*', in Santaolalla et al. (2004: 397–404).

Perrier, Jean-Louis (1970). 'L'oeil tranché', *Cinéthique* 7–8.

Piazza, Francois (1949). 'Considerations psychanalytiques sur *Le (sic) chien andalou* de Luis Buñuel et Salvador Dalí', *Psyche* 27–28: 147–56.

Pierre, José, ed. (1992). *Investigating Sex: Surrealist Research 1928–1932*, trans. Malcolm Imrie (London and New York: WW. Norton and Co. Ltd.)

Piqueras, Jean (1929). 'Cinema de vanguardia: *Un perro andaluz*', *Popular Film* (Barcelona) (1 August).

Powrie, Phil (1998). 'Masculinity in the Shadow of the Slashed Eye: Surrealist Film Criticism at the Crossroads', *Screen* 39(2): 153–63.

Puig Pujades, Josep (1929). 'Un film a Figueres. Una idea de Salvador Dalí i Luís Buñuel', *La Veu de l'Empordà* (2 February).

Puyal, Alfonso (1999). '"Vaya Marista!": La version literaria de *Un perro andaluz*', *Cuadernos de la Acadamia* 5 (May), 237–55.

Radford, Robert (1997). *Dali* (London: Phaidon).

Raeburn, Michael. ed. (1994). *Salvador Dalí: The Early Years* (London: South Bank Centre).

Ramain, Paul (1925). 'L'Influence du rêve sur le cinéma', *Cinéa-Ciné pour tous* 40: 8; trans. Abel (1988: 362–4).

Renaud, Pierre (1963). 'Symbolisme au second degré: *Un chien andalou*', *Etudes cinématographiques*, 22–23: 147–57.

'Revue des revues' (1929). *La Revue du cinéma* 1(5): 77–8.

Roberts, Marie Louise (1994). *Civilization without Sexes: Reconstructing Gender in Postwar France 1917–1927* (Chicago and London: Chicago University Press).

Sadoul, Georges (1949). *Histoire du cinéma mondial, des origines à nos jours* (Paris: Flammarion).

Sadoul, Georges (1962). 'Buñuel, *Viridiana*, et quelques autres', preface to *Luis Buñuel. Viridiana* (Paris: InterSpectacles).

Sánchez Vidal, Agustín (1988). *Buñuel, Lorca, Dalí: El Enigma Sin Fin* (Barcelona: Planeta).

Sánchez Vidal, Agustín (1994). 'The Andalusian beasts', in Raeburn (1994: 193–207).

Sandro, Paul (1987). *Diversions of Pleasure. Luis Buñuel and the Crises of Desire* (Ohio State University Press).

Santaolalla, Isabel et al., eds. (2004) *Buñuel, siglo XXI* (Prensas Universitarias de Zaragoza).

Short, Robert (2002). *The Age of Gold. Surrealist Cinema* (London: Creation Books).

Siegel, Jeanne (1982). 'The Image of the Eye in Surrealist Art and its Psychoanalytical Sources', *Arts Magazine* 56(6): 102–6.

Smith, Paul Julian (1995). 'Shocks and Prejudices', *Sight and Sound* 5(8): 24–6.

Sontag, Susan (1981). *Styles of Radical Will* (New York: Picador USA).

Soupault, Philippe (1979). *Ecrits de cinéma* (Paris: Plon).

*Le Surréalisme et le cinéma* (1965). *Etudes cinématographiques*, 38–39 and 40–42.

Suleiman, Susan Rubin (1990). *Subversive Intent. Gender, Politics, and the Avant-Garde* (Cambridge Mass. and London: Harvard University Press).

Talens, Jenaro (1993). *The Branded Eye. Buñuel's 'Un chien andalou'* (Minneapolis: University of Minnesota Press).

Thévenet, Jean (1930). 'Mickey et *Un chien andalou*, *L'Autorité* (Brussels) (20 March).

Thiher, Allen (1979). *The Cinematic Muse: Critical Studies in the History of French Cinema* (Columbia and London: University of Missouri Press).

Tual, Denise (1987). *Au Coeur du temps* (Paris: Carrère).

Turrent, Tomás Pérez and José de la Colina (1993). *Conversations avec Luis Buñuel. Il est dangereux de se pencher au-dedans* (Paris: Cahiers du Cinéma).

Vaizey, Marina (1979). 'The irritating genius of Salvador Dali', *The Sunday Times* (30 December).

Vigo, Jean (1930). 'Un chien andalou hurle', *Ciné-Club* 5; trans. Drummond in Buñuel and Dalí (1994: xxv–xxvi).

Virmaux, Alain and Odette (1976). *Les Surréalistes et le cinéma. Anthologie* (Paris: Seghers).

Walker, Ian (1977). 'Once upon a time…', *Sight and Sound* 47(1): 2–5.

Walz, Robin (2000). *Pulp Surrealism: Insolent Popular Culture in Early Twentieth-Century Paris* (Berkeley, Los Angeles, London: University of California Press).

Williams, Linda (1976). 'The Prologue in *Un chien andalou*: A Surrealist Film Metaphor', *Screen*, 17(4): 24–33.

Williams, Linda (1981a). *Figures of Desire. A Theory and Analysis of Surrealist Film* (Urbana: University of Illinois Press).

Williams, Linda (1981b). 'Dream Rhetoric and Film Rhetoric: Metaphor and Metonymy in *Un chien andalou*', *Semiotica*, 33(1–2): 87–103.

Williams, Linda (1991). 'Film Bodies: Gender, Genre, and Excess', *Film Quarterly* 44(4): 2–13.

Williams, Linda (1994). 'An Eye for an Eye', *Sight and Sound* 14(4): 15–16.

Williams, Linda, ed. (1995). *Viewing Positions. Ways of Seeing Film* (Rutgers University Press).

Williams, Linda (1996). 'The critical grasp: Buñuelian cinema and its critics', in Kuenzli (1996: 199–206).

www.ingramcontent.com/pod-product-compliance
Lightning Source LLC
LaVergne TN
LVHW020644100826
845148LV00012B/2336

* 9 7 8 1 8 4 8 8 5 0 5 6 9 *